The Mythologizing of Mark Twain

The Mythologizing of
MARK TWAIN

EDITED BY

Sara deSaussure Davis

AND

Philip D. Beidler

THE UNIVERSITY OF ALABAMA PRESS

Permission to reproduce the Norman Rockwell illustrations is gratefully acknowledged as follows:

Tom Sawyer whitewashing the fence (1), Huck showing Tom the
dead cat (2), Tom gets a whipping (3), and Tom and Huck and Joe on
Jackson's Island (4) from *Adventures of Tom Sawyer*, illustrated by
Norman Rockwell, © 1936 by The Heritage Club (MBI, Inc.). Used
by permission.

Pap waiting for Huck in his room (5), Jim listening to hair-ball oracle (6), Huck disguised as Sarah/Mary Williams (7), and first illustration of the King and the Duke, showing the Mississippi River
(8) from *Adventures of Huckleberry Finn*, illustrated by Norman
Rockwell, © 1940 by The Heritage Club (MBI, Inc.). Used by
permission.

SECOND PAPERBACK PRINTING 1986

Library of Congress Cataloging in Publication Data

Main entry under title:
The Mythologizing of Mark Twain.

Essays presented at the Eighth Alabama Symposium on English and American
Literature, Oct. 15–17, 1981, University of Alabama.
Includes index.
1. Twain, Mark, 1835–1910—Criticism and interpretation—Congresses.
I. Davis, Sara deSaussure, 1943–
II. Beidler, Philip D.
PS1338.M9 1984   818'.409   83-9166
ISBN 0-8173-0199-2
ISBN 0-8173-0201-8 (pbk.)

In memory of
Ruth Tisdale Wilder
1941–1981
beloved friend and colleague

Contents

Illustrations

The Mythologizing of Mark Twain

Sara deSaussure Davis

Introduction

The question of Mark Twain's worth as a writer has been an intriguing and problematical issue since he began his literary career in the 1860s, when the debate was largely a matter of whether he was just another funny fellow or a serious author. With protean vitality, the forms of the issue have changed but refuse to resolve themselves into answers or to vanish. So we are left with this nagging contradiction: We accept Mark Twain as a major American writer—perhaps even as our most typically native product—at the same time that we register our disappointment over his recently published *Notebooks,* which read, as Harold Kolb says, like the jottings of a journalist.[1] That is to say, not like an artist's, not like a "true" writer's. Or we think of Hemingway's nearly untempered admiration for Twain's masterpiece, *The Adventures of Huckleberry Finn,* when he said that all American literature came from that rich source yet warned readers to stop at the point in the narrative where Tom Sawyer arrives at the Phelps farm. That is to say, even his best work is seriously flawed, though from generation to generation we disagree even about what those flaws are. One symptom of the current fluctuation in values regarding Twain is the intense debate among scholars over the significance of his late works, those written after about 1898. There seems no middle ground: While conventional scholarly wisdom has deemed these mostly unfinished and unpublished pieces inferior, other critics proclaim them brilliant and successful. Few serious readers of Twain doubt his genius, but defining and locating the source of his genius continue to challenge scholars, as does the attempt to explain the apparent discrepancy between the enormity of his fame and the unevenness of his literary production.

This volume's eight essays respond variously to the complexity of the mythologizing of Mark Twain. The mythologizing posits, in one sense, that Americans have raised Samuel Clemens, for whatever reasons or necessities, to the level of myth, where he embodies our idea of ourselves. But what were the necessities of such a transformation? We could say that it was inevitable, if we listen to de Tocqueville, who predicted so much from his 1830s visit to America:

> Taken as a whole, literature in democratic ages can never present, as it does in the periods of aristocracy, an aspect of order, regularity, science, and art; its form, on the contrary, will ordinarily be slighted, sometimes despised. Style will frequently be fantastic, incorrect, overburdened, and loose, almost always vehement and bold. Authors will aim at rapidity of execution more than at perfection of detail. Small productions will be more common than bulky books; there will be more wit than erudition, more imagination than profundity; and literary performances will bear marks of an untutored and rude vigor of thought, frequently of great variety and singular fecundity. The object of authors will be to astonish rather than to please, and to stir the passions more than to charm the taste.[2]

So, then, the political and social realities inherent in American life may have predicated an artist like Mark Twain, warts and all.

The process of myth making is not one way or passive, however. Twain actively participated in his own creation, thanks partly to the development of the American newspaper interview, which Twain was a master in exploiting. Louis Budd and Henry Nash Smith reveal the degree to which Twain promoted his own actions in the newspapers by assiduously cultivating and amusing reporters, by stage-managing his appearances. Twain may have practiced, as he said, an unconscious form of writing, but he was acutely self-conscious in the cultivation of his public image, so that while we may laugh at some of our contemporary forms of Twain worship outlined in John Gerber's paper, we are forced to recognize that most of the artifacts are in keeping with what Twain might have done for himself. In fact, we might wonder, as Alan Gribben does, whether such a life as Twain's is more significant than his art. To assume this, however, is to assume that his art might have been possible without his life as it was.

The myth-making process, whether shaped unconsciously by the American public or consciously by Twain himself, of course works in the direction of enlargement, of enhancement, but simultaneously the myth defines and delimits. In his study of the contemporary newspaper accounts of Twain, Henry Nash Smith analyzes the forces within American culture that stereotyped and thus handicapped Twain in his efforts to address serious issues. Serious literature and humor, especially of the "low" sort practiced by Westerners and lecture performers like Twain, were mutually exclusive when judged by the intolerant standards of the Genteel Tradition, the forces of highbrow culture, as Smith has termed it in his *Democracy and the Novel*.[3]

The enduring contours of the myth of Twain the man emerged clearly in 1900, when he returned triumphantly to America after his worldwide lecture tour of 1895/96 and his residence abroad. He had repaid his debts, so that this homecoming, biographer Justin Kaplan makes clear, was one stage of a career that fit "a mythic pattern of journey from poverty and obscurity, of mortal struggle, and of victory and return."[4] While the universality of this heroic pattern is obvious, there is a decidedly American quality to it in that Twain's struggle was specifically the fight to manipulate the almighty dollar into millions. His bankruptcy would surely have engaged both the pity and fear of most Americans; but such a tragedy would have been out of keeping with the spirit of the times. That he recovered a respectable portion of his wealth and repaid to the penny his debts ennobled both the failure and the man, in the public's view, and restored its stalwart optimism. "The Hero as Man of Letters," proclaimed a newspaper of the day.[5]

Perhaps the most accessible avenue to self-definition, to finding one's place in the supposedly loose social structure of democratic America was financial success, and as we look over the proliferation, even the squandering of Twain's energies in pursuing his

place, de Tocqueville's analysis of our society again offers a pre-
scient description of Twain. In answering "why the Americans are
more addicted to practical than to theoretical science," de Tocqueville writes, "Everyone is in motion, some in quest of power, others of gain. In the midst of this universal tumult, this incessant conflict of jarring interests, this continual striving of men after fortune,
where is that calm to be found which is necessary for the deeper
combinations of the intellect? How can the mind dwell upon any
single point when everything whirls around it, and man himself is
swept and beaten onwards by the heady current that rolls all things
in its course?"[6]

But Twain embodies not only the quintessentially American
myth of success; he seems, like Ben Franklin before him, to have
encompassed all the major aspects of American life during his century. As Arthur Pettit has pointed out, "The list of his [Twain's] personal experiences reads like a table of contents for a textbook in
nineteenth-century American history: Slavery in the Border South;
Life on the Mississippi; The House Divided; The Civil War; the
Frontier West; Reconstruction; The American Innocent Abroad;
the Industrial Revolution; The Politics of Business; The Gilded
Age."[7] We Americans have always valued the person who has "been
there," who has seen, experienced, and therefore known the "real
thing." It's all very well for Henry James to advise young writers
that it is not necessary to have experienced something physically in
order to write about it convincingly, so long as they can imagine it
concretely; but as Americans we are more the inheritors of William
than of Henry James: we like the authenticity of pragmatic effects,
the red badges of courage. We like someone who's been there.
Who better, then, to know the effects of commercial venture and
investment than the man who sank thousands of dollars into the
Paige typesetting machine and the health-food supplement, Plas-
mon (to name only two of his investments)? Who better to know,
and thus to write of, the boom-bust mentality of America than
young Sam Clemens, who was there in the silver mines of the
West? Who better to imagine our childhood than a man who, as
William Dean Howells said, remained a youth all his life?

Twain was very much aware of the significant connection between himself and his times, as a notebook entry at the turn of
the century expresses clearly: "The 20th century is a stranger to

me. . . . I wish it well but my heart is all for my own century. I took 65 years of it, just on risk, but if I had known as much about it as I know now I would have taken the whole of it."[8] Twain's ardor for the nineteenth century was mutual: a lover's embrace, and each saw the world reflected in the other's eye. The rapport with his times was usually so privileged that he could laugh at them, satirize them with the impunity of a Jew telling a Jewish joke. Only later—the sense of disjunction Twain registers in this notebook entry is but one symptom—did he wholeheartedly revile the times, human nature, and America, though he was careful to suppress most of these attacks and defer them to posthumous publication. Or, as Stanley Brodwin shows, Twain devised elaborate strategies to disguise his cultural and cosmic irreverence.

As the times mythologized Twain, so Twain transformed his life's experiences into cultural myth—such myths of our national experience as that of the West, analyzed by Harold H. Kolb, and that of the river, explored by James Cox. Brodwin, Kolb, and Cox explicitly and implicitly confirm that Twain's genius transcends the dangers to his art posed by the forces within American society and within his own psyche. In fact, his genius transcended these forces and dangers best by transforming and incorporating them into his work. As one German scholar of Twain puts it, "Twain was a genius where he had the courage and honesty to let the disruptive elements appear in all their disruptiveness and where he made his own process of doubting and wavering part of the artistic structure, as he did in *Huck Finn* and especially in *A Connecticut Yankee*."[9]

Twain served, as Ezra Pound said of poets, as the antennae of his race, experiencing and sensing those characteristics of life that would emerge more clearly in another generation or two. Praising *The Gilded Age* as "our best political novel," for example, Garry Wills says: "To understand America, read Mark Twain. If I believed in sortilege, Twain's would have to be my holy books. No matter what new craziness pops up in America, I find it described beforehand by him."[10]

There are many paradoxes in Clemens the man, in Twain the writer, but one pertinent to the question at hand is that although Twain was bound up so intimately with the affairs of his times— seemingly one of the last major American writers to be so—by the turn of the century he also began to experience what has now become a cliché version of the twentieth-century artist: a figure divorced from the times, isolated by protest or temperament or resignation from government and business and society. After his return from Europe in 1900, his writings and his ideas were so out of harmony with prevailing American views that he could maintain his popularity only by protecting the public image of Mark Twain. He could continue writing only by consigning most of his manuscripts to a posthumous file, to be published one hundred years after his death. Or he could write only in fits and spurts, unable to sustain an idea to completion, to a structural whole.

While we may look with some superiority on the adulation of Twain's contemporaries for him—especially by those who took the man as a humorist and nothing more "serious," or those who responded primarily to his platform personality and newspaper image—the worship in our own time has neither abated nor limited itself to the populace. One measure of the attitude that Twain is merely an entertainer is apparent in the Norman Rockwell illustrations of *Adventures of Huckleberry Finn* and *The Adventures of Tom Sawyer,* which, as Allison Ensor demonstrates, parallel the attitude of the American public toward Twain: the darker side of human nature is missing. Another measure of the same sentimentalizing effacement reveals itself periodically in various television and movie adaptations of Twain's work. One recent example is the 1980 production of "The Man That Corrupted Hadleyburg." As dramatized on PBS, which draws a far more sophisticated audience than the commercial networks, the fable's moral pith and vinegar have been neutralized, so that Twain's vision of greed, of secret sin, of cowardice, conformity, and remorse is simplified into a concoction as bland as instant grits. For what purpose though? Expediency? The nature of the medium? Public expectation—*still*—about the boy's-tale author, "the funniest man in the world"? Henry Nash Smith, in his essay for this volume, has analyzed how the failure of Twain's culture to understand the source of his literary power handicapped his abilities; but what excuse do we have in the twentieth century?

Scholars (and professional reviewers) too have produced Twain worshipers—"the Idolators," Hamlim Hill calls them in a recent review[11]—who protest against the unpleasant revelations concerning Twain's life and/or against low critical estimates of his later works. It is ironic that simultaneously academia is producing, on the one hand, worshipers, who help solidify a stereotype of Twain by ignoring or stripping away vital details of his life and work like excresences that needn't count, and on the other hand an abundance of riches by way of publication of Twain's notebooks and journals, new and authoritative editions of his works, new biographical studies on heretofore less-studied aspects of his life.[12] The scholars involved in this counterpoint seem like the chicks of the great hornbilled birds of Africa. Two sibling birds, born twenty-four hours apart in a hole plastered shut by their mother, instinctively pursue diametrically opposed actions: the firstborn pecks away at the plastered hole to enlarge it and so escape; while the other as assiduously keeps replastering the hole, until its time for freedom comes. Both birds survive, and the huge, magical baobab tree in which this drama occurs seems like Twain himself—able to support many apparently contradictory forms of life simultaneously.

AMERICA

MYTHOLOGIZES

TWAIN

John C. Gerber

Collecting the
Works of Mark Twain

The current scramble for Twainiana is a sign—and a telling one—
of the larger-than-life position that Mark Twain has come to occupy
in our culture. Mark Twain collectors vary in age from ten to
ninety, in economic status from young students with just enough
spare change to buy an 1898 reprint to business and professional
persons willing to pay $3,000 or more for a first printing, in com-
mitment from casual collectors who buy a single work on impulse
to ferrets who haunt the bookstores and plague the dealers by mail
for the works they most need to fill out their extensive holdings.

Booksellers confirm this extraordinary interest in collecting
Mark Twain material. Several years ago, J. W. Warnick wrote in
the *Book Collector's Market* that, with the possible exceptions of
Steinbeck and Faulkner, Mark Twain is "the most collected American author today."[1] Recently, two booksellers, Van Allen Bradley of
Scottsdale, Arizona, and Warren R. Howell of San Francisco both
wrote me that there is a strong and continuing demand for Mark
Twain books. David Holmes of George S. MacManus Company in
Philadelphia goes further in saying that "except for truly excep-
tional items only Melville has rivalled Twain in increased interest
over the past few years." He adds that Twain, in his opinion,
has won over the greatest number of enthusiastic collectors.
"The Longfellows, Hawthornes, Emersons, Lowells, etc. have not
moved ahead much at all." Willis Monie of Cooperstown, New

York, puts it in a letter to me still more sweepingly: he finds Twain to be "the most collected, by far, of American authors, and, in this country at least, of all authors."

Why this extraordinary demand? Why are so many people collecting the works of Mark Twain? Some of the reasons apply to collecting of all kinds. Collecting has been, and is, a common human trait; witness the old license plates nailed to garage walls, the beer cans displayed on shelves in wood-paneled dens, the unnumbered accumulations of string, buttons, dolls, baseball cards, theater programs, and *National Geographics*, as well as collections of stamps and coins, books, and works of art. Hamlin Garland kept menus and theater stubs, and just the other day I heard of two characters who vie with each other in collecting steel tractor seats.

Doubtless there is a dissertation written in some sociology department that learnedly spells out the economic, psychological, educational, and social factors responsible for collecting, and how collecting may be seen as an index of cultural trends. More simply, we may mention here such causes as the desire for unique possessions, the excitement of the search, the drive of competition, and the delight of showing off one's acquisitions. For collectors turned investors, moreover, there is the hope that a collection of Prendergasts or silver dollars or the novels of Edgar Rice Burroughs may serve as a hedge against inflation. Such general considerations, however, do not account for the special popularity of Mark Twain materials. Why collect *these*? Let me offer three reasons.

One reason must surely be the continuing popularity of Mark Twain himself. His pictures continue to appear in newspapers and magazines, and he continues to be quoted and alluded to in books and articles and TV programs of almost every description. Nor is his popularity limited to this country, for he is still one of the two or three best-known and most widely read American authors abroad. Two years ago, when I had the happy opportunity to lecture to students majoring in English in universities in Peking, Nanking, and Shanghai, it was Mark Twain they wanted to hear about—not just Tom Sawyer and Huckleberry Finn but the author himself.

Possibly the surest proof of continuing popularity is the fact that he is still being exploited commercially. One may sniff at such exploitation, but it would not occur if the man were not well known and widely respected: a legend, if you will. In the past, advertisers have used his picture in spreads for such items as cigars, collars, sardines, flour, health food, billiard tables, and Campbell's soup. More recently they have used him to popularize Old Crow and both McCormick and Mark Twain distilleries, beer mugs, dolls, plates, calendars, and Tennessee Gas. The owners of the *Delta Queen* invariably include his picture in advertisements for their Mississippi River cruises, and the makers of a new card game for youngsters have been featuring his picture, along with those of Washington and Lincoln. His likeness also appears on one of four medallions struck by the U.S. Mint. Approximately 70,000 persons visit his former home in Hartford every year, and 200,000 his former home in Hannibal.

To repeat, this kind of exploitation would not be engaged in if Mark Twain were not a legend in our time. As a legend, Mark Twain is alive and well—and almost as well known as he ever was.

In addition, many collect his books simply because they are attractive on their library shelves. First editions of Emerson and Hawthorne merely blacken the room, and those of Howells and James don't exactly brighten the place. But Mark Twain's American editions, sold by the subscription method, had to be not only substantial in size but eye catching in appearance. The housewife, before buying it, wanted to know how a volume would look on her parlor table. The agents of the American Publishing Company, Osgood, and Charles L. Webster and Company, Mark Twain's chief publishers in the nineteenth century, were prepared not only to tell her but to show her. They would produce a prospectus containing samples of cloth and leather bindings, gold stampings, engravings, and enough of the text to reveal how readable the type was.

Although they did not use the word, so far as I know, subscription publishers in the nineteenth century knew how to "package" their products to make them sell. As a result, a row of Mark Twain's first editions is still a delight to see, ranging from the black and gold of *Innocents Abroad* and *Roughing It*, through the green or blue of *Tom Sawyer* and *Huckleberry Finn,* with their gold and black ornamental designs, to the light green cloth and gorgeous gold and blue stampings of *A Connecticut Yankee* and the rich brown cloth and gold lettering of *Pudd'nhead Wilson*. If some of these are bound in half-calf or morocco, so much the better. Even the earliest book, *The Celebrated Jumping Frog of Calaveras*

County, and Other Sketches, not published by a subscription house, appears in a variety of colors, with a gold vignette of a frog on the front cover staring determinedly at the upper right-hand corner or, more rarely, in the lower middle staring up just as determinedly at the title. In *Life on the Mississippi,* J. W. Warnick observes, we see "the pinnacle of American book design." He also praises the scrollwork on the cover of *The Prince and the Pauper.*[2]

Though less varied and somewhat less attractive, English editions add further color, especially the Chatto and Windus books, bound in scarlet with black and gold lettering that vaguely suggests Egyptian hieroglyphics. Canadian and Leipzig editions, usually bound in more somber colors, by that very fact add variety, thereby gratifying a number of collectors who keep adding Mark Twain books, in part to apply greater brightness and variety to the palette on their book shelves.

A third reason for the current activity in the market for Mark Twain materials is that, despite the dwindling supply, there is still much to be found, especially for those who are willing to extend their search beyond first printings of the best-known books. Jacob Blanck lists 277 Mark Twain primary books and books that contain first-edition material.[3] Such figures are just the start. Many of these editions appeared in several printings and some of the printings in several states. For example, the text of *Roughing It,* published in 1872, was not reset until 1900; instead, the American Publishing Company issued ten reprintings of the first setting. Thus, though copies of the first state of the first printing are hard to find, copies of other states and printings of the first edition are not particularly elusive. After all, close to 100,000 of them were printed. Similarly, while the first states of *Innocents Abroad, Tom Sawyer,* and the other major works are rare—and expensive when they are found—collectors, even those of modest means, can put together substantial collections of later states and printings.

The Mark Twain market includes much more than American books, however. There are all the early printings of foreign editions, not only English, Canadian, and the German editions in English but the many translations into foreign languages as well. The prospectuses are at present an especially hot item, albeit expensive. Collectors who have the facilities for storing them properly can still find magazines and newspapers that carry original Mark

Twain material—not copies of the *Territorial Enterprise*, to be sure, but such prominent publications as the *Atlantic, Century,* and *Cosmopolitan*. For the persistent collector, also, occasionally such odds and ends are available as autographs, letters, photographs, auction catalogues, banquet and lecture programs, and books and household items Mark Twain owned. Finally, for those with stout hearts and deformed consciences are all the books and articles *about* the author. Thomas A. Tenney, in his extraordinarily useful *Mark Twain: A Reference Guide* and in the supplements that have appeared since 1977, lists some 16,750 of them—and about fifty more come out every year.[4]

The real excitement, however, is in the competition for early states of first printings of first American editions (for simplicity's sake I shall usually call these versions "firsts"). Whether one can afford these firsts or not, they are the items that almost all Mark Twain collectors covet, the works that evoke their deepest interest, the not-so-holy grails for which they joust, the prizes for which they may have to give up a vacation or a new car. To get into this competition these days, one must have patience, tenacity, money, and not a little idiocy. This competition is "hard ball" whereas the rest of it is good clean fun.

What is happening, of course, is that swelling numbers of collectors, including wealthy business and professional persons, are competing for a diminishing supply of the earliest states of American editions. One never *writes* any longer for a copy of a first printing listed in a catalogue—never writes, that is, if he or she really wants the item. Even by telephone, in my experience, one has only one chance in four or five of getting what one wants, and no chance at all if the item is rare. Mr. Monie comments that if he gets a fine copy of one of the scarcer items, he cannot hold it long enough to catalogue it. Even asking a dealer to search for a book is no guarantee of success: Van Allen Bradley this past year has been able to obtain only 35 of 202 items on his Mark Twain "want list."

It is not surprising, therefore, that prices have skyrocketed. If proof of this is needed, let me rank a score or more works according to the prices listed in Van Allen Bradley's most recent *Handbook*.[5] These are all prices asked for cloth-bound copies without dust jackets, and do not include autographed or otherwise eccentric copies. Interestingly, not all of the titles are the familiar ones.

Up to $5,000   *The Celebrated Jumping Frog of Calaveras*
                County, The Adventures of Tom Sawyer
Up to $2,500   *Adventures of Huckleberry Finn, Pudd'nhead Wilson's Calendar for 1894*
Up to $1,200   *The Gilded Age*
Up to $1,000   *Tom Sawyer Abroad, Tom Sawyer Detective, and Other Stories*
Up to $800   *A True Story; Be Good, Be Good: A Poem*
Up to $750   *Innocents Abroad, Life on the Mississippi*
Up to $600   *Number One: Mark Twain's Sketches. Authorized Edition, Facts for Mark Twain's Memory Builder*
Up to $550   *The Prince and the Pauper*
Up to $500   *A Murder, A Mystery, and A Marriage*
Up to $450   *A Tramp Abroad, Queen Victoria's Jubilee*
Up to $400   *Roughing It, Old Times on the Mississippi, Pudd'nhead Wilson, Eye Openers*
Up to $350   *A Connecticut Yankee in King Arthur's Court; Punch, Brothers, Punch!*
Up to $300   *A Curious Dream, The Mysterious Stranger, To the Person Sitting in Darkness, Tom Sawyer Abroad*

Mr. Holmes tells me that many of the first printings in the lower price range have increased in cost even more dramatically, sometimes by a factor of ten. Thus Alan C. Fox, a dealer in Sherman Oaks, California, asked, and got, $200 for a copy of *Nightmare;* $400 for a copy of *Sketches, New and Old;* and $800 for a copy of *A True Story and the Recent Carnival of Crime.* The cost of offbeat items has kept pace. Fox received $450 for a printer's dummy of *The £1,000,000 Bank-Note,* and asked $4,250 for a prospectus of *A Connecticut Yankee* and $5,750 for one of *Huckleberry Finn.* These latter items he ultimately turned over to the Heritage Bookshop in Los Angeles, which promptly discounted them by 30 percent, but even so, the price of $2,975 for *Yankee* represents a very considerable jump from the $600 asked by John Howell–Books five years ago, especially since the Heritage volume lacks a sample of the half-morocco backstrip and all of the order sheets.

Why this passion for the earliest states of first American editions? Why will a buyer pay $1,200 for a copy of *The Gilded Age,* bearing the date 1873, when for $15 he or she might find one dated 1874 that in most respects is identical, even to calling Colonel Sellers "Eschol" rather than "Beriah"? Are there rational reasons for such behavior?

There are reasons that I can offer, of course, but they will have to be speculative. I have talked with collectors and booksellers and have tried to identify my own motives in buying an occasional first. But what follows is a series of hunches which lead me to conclude that no material reason, economic or otherwise, fully accounts for the current demand for firsts, and, therefore, that we are forced to assume that the firsts have taken on a mystique, a legendary quality, an appeal that quite transcends material matters. But first, to the material matters.

1. *Investment*. At least in the back of the minds of most buyers of firsts, I suspect, is the notion of investment. First editions in fine condition have increased in value dramatically in the last ten years or so, and no American works more than Mark Twain's. His is probably the most active market, as we have seen, and, therefore, the one in which prices are most likely to continue bullish, at least for the foreseeable future. So a collection of first printings of such works as *Tom Sawyer, Huckleberry Finn,* and *The Jumping Frog* may very well be a shrewd hedge against inflation.

Yet most collectors I know consider investment only a subsidiary reason for buying Mark Twain firsts. In buying a book, dealers normally pay only half of what they hope to get for the book. Hence if collectors pay $100 for a book today, they can count on getting only $50 for it tomorrow. The market value for the work will have to double before the initial investment is returned, in dollars that will probably be worth less. Before a collector can receive an appreciable return, therefore, market values have to triple. In short, a collector (as investor) who pays $1,000 for a first printing of *Tom Sawyer* in very fine condition is betting that its value will ultimately be at least $3,000. ("Ultimately" could mean ten years—or twenty.) The person who is out to improve his or her nest egg quickly would be far better advised to buy bank certificates or Treasury bills, and I suspect most book collectors know it. The current demand for firsts, therefore, can be attributed in part to economic motives, but by no means entirely so.

2. *Manufacture*. Also, the demand can be attributed in part to a desire for superior physical products, but only in part. Collectors who fancy themselves as highly discriminating insist on early states because they believe that they are superior physically. To be sure, impressions on sheets that rolled off the press first are likely to be sharper than impressions on reprints. There is no denying that with continued use the plates wore down, as did the stamps used for the lettering and designs on the cover. But as for other aspects of manufacture the firsts seem to have no advantages, even for the most discriminating buyers.

To put this another way, there is little or no evidence that the American Publishing Company, Osgood, or Webster lavished special care and expense on the first run of an edition. One gets the feeling that, regardless of the printing, the printers and binders did what was handiest at the moment. A first printing, for example, may be on laid or wove paper, or even on both (indeed, a single copy may be on both). Books in a first printing may be sewn or stapled. The fact that early copies of *Huckleberry Finn* appeared in both green and blue cloth carries no significance with respect to the quality of the book *qua* book. Those in blue bring higher prices simply because they are scarcer. Gold and sprinkled edges, half-calf and half-morocco bindings, were available to those who were willing to pay a higher tariff, regardless of the printing.

My point is that, except for sharpness of impression, almost no case can be made for the notion that the firsts are superior physical products. I doubt that many collectors consider this a major reason for buying firsts.

3. *Curiosities*. Many especially enjoy the first states of first printings because they contain the major curiosities and bloopers. It's in the earliest state or states, for example, that the tablecloth appears in the frontispiece of *Huckleberry Finn* and that Uncle Silas' famous fly is either properly closed or hilariously open, or again closed on a new page that has been tipped in. It's in first state, too, that in *Life on the Mississippi* the St. Charles Hotel is miscaptioned and that the head of Mark Twain appears engulfed in flames—an engraving that so dismayed Mrs. Clemens that she ordered it excised. Such curiosities are amusing enough for above-average cocktail chatter, but I doubt that many collectors pay a thousand dollars more for a copy of *Life on the Mississippi* just be-

cause it shows Mark Twain's head in flames. The real value of these abnormalities is that they signal the first state, but most collectors value the first state primarily for other reasons.

4. *Authoritativeness*. Unthinkable as it may be to scholars, there are collectors, especially outside the academic community, who still believe that the first state of the first printing of the first American edition of a Mark Twain work is the most authoritative. They reason that the firsts are the versions that Mark Twain edited and proofread, that he must have seen through the press, and therefore reflect most accurately what he wanted. It often comes as an enormous surprise to such people to learn this is not the case. They are really shaken, for example, to discover that the first nine chapters of the first American printing of *Tom Sawyer Abroad* contain scores of alterations imposed by Mary Mapes Dodge when she "purified" the text for the little innocents who read her *St. Nicholas*. One would like to think that almost everyone knows that the Iowa-California editions are *the* most authoritative versions, but— alas—such is not the case.

5. *Rarity*. Rarity is a far more significant reason for the demand for firsts. There is no doubt that American firsts in fine, very fine, and mint condition are scarce and are becoming scarcer—and hence more desirable. The reasons are simple. Being the oldest versions, an especially high proportion of them have deteriorated badly and/or have been pitched into the rubbish barrel. Of those that remain unscathed by age and handling, most now stand on shelves in rare-book rooms in university or public libraries, or in libraries of collectors who intend to keep them indefinitely and, in many instances, to bequeath them ultimately to institutions. Some dealers keep these books themselves or give them to relatives. So the number coming on the open market, or likely to come on the market in the future, is highly restricted.

In 1981 the Heritage Bookshop announced a sale of five hundred Mark Twain works, most of them first editions (a major collector had decided to sell his holdings); but such an event is infrequent these days. Those who seek firsts, and especially those who seek particular firsts to fill gaps in their collections, may go years without finding the books they want. The capture of such a book thus becomes a great triumph over odds, a demonstration of perseverance and grit and luck.

The rarity of a book undoubtedly adds edge to the search, and drives up the demand—and the price—yet, extraordinary as it may seem, rarity is not a thoroughly trustworthy determinant of value, for the rarest works are not always the most sought after. English firsts are on the whole scarcer than American firsts, though only occasionally does an English publication of Twain command a price comparable to the price for its American counterpart. Copies from the first American printing of *Tom Sawyer* are scarcer than copies of the first American printing of *Huckleberry Finn;* yet the latter book is priced above the former in most catalogues.

One of the rarest books is the Harper edition of *Tom Sawyer Abroad, Tom Sawyer Detective, and Other Stories* (1896); yet even Alan Fox in his recent catalogue asked only a third as much for a mint copy of it as for fine copies of *Tom Sawyer* and *Huckleberry Finn.* And he asked only $200 for a Routledge reprint of the *Jumping Frog* in pictorial wrappers, which is probably rarer than any American first. Examples could be multiplied. The point is that, important as it is, neither collectors nor dealers use rarity as a sole determinant of value.

6. *The Demand Itself.* The demand for Mark Twain firsts is undoubtedly in part the result of a bandwagon effect. Demand builds up demand. Persons who never thought of collecting Mark Twain firsts want to get into the game because so many others are playing it. High prices give copies of first printings a cachet or an aura of splendor, if not a snob value. We are so accustomed to accepting a price as an index of value that we act like Pavlov's famous hound. Because diamonds cost more at Cartier's than at the Acme Discount House, the former must be better; a salesman once told me that he could not persuade customers to buy an $18 radio instead of a $29 version, even when he demonstrated that the components were identical.

One of the first things an enthusiastic collector will tell you in displaying a copy of a first printing he has just bought is how high the price for it has gone up. (I use the masculine pronoun here but I could just as accurately use the feminine.) He may be a bit sheepish in admitting he paid $800 for a book, but he will try to dazzle you with the figure nevertheless. He will be positively triumphant, however, if he can tell you that a friend paid $800, whereas *he* found a copy for $350. In either case, the $800 figure gets top billing as an index of value.

Prices, of course, are not the initial cause of the passion for firsts. Without a demand, dealers could not push up their prices as they have: the greater the demand, the higher the prices—of course. But ironically, the higher the prices, the more transcendentally attractive the firsts become and, hence, the greater the demand.

7. *Mystique*. Now we get into the world of intangibles and will have to tread gingerly. Of the material factors responsible for the passion for early states of first printings, we have seen that none, by itself, is wholly decisive—not even rarity. One is tempted, therefore, to conclude that the demand is due in every instance to a combination of these tangibles: investment possibilities, the capture of an endangered species, sharpness of impression, and so on. But the truth is that even the most favorable combination of tangibles fails to account completely for the adoration collectors reveal for their firsts.

Typical Mark Twain collectors, showing off their books, will apologize for a copy of a second edition, and even let the guest's young son leaf through it to see the engravings. A first edition, second printing, however, receives more careful treatment. The son is kept at a safe distance, and only the adult guest may hold the book and leaf through it, and as soon as politeness permits, the owner retrieves the volume and puts it back on the shelf. But even the adult guest, however responsible, is unlikely to be allowed to handle a first state of the first printing. The owner holds it delicately, as though dealing with the Host at the altar, and tells of its distinctive and distinguishing characteristics in a voice almost taut with emotion. Then, with consummate care, the collector quickly returns it to its honored place behind a glass door.

No combination of tangibles can account for such reverence, even the outrageous price that may have been paid. Clearly, the whole is greater than the sum of the parts. The earliest state enjoys a mystique possessed by no other version. Why? Let me try three brief answers.

The American first seems to get us closer to the author than the other versions. Perhaps it is not the most authoritative, but it is the version that Mark Twain worried through the press, that excited him most, that he showed off to his family and friends. The bloopers in it are the ones that infuriated him and annoyed Mrs. Clemens. Firsts, in short, exude a sense of the captious, drawling author who created them—as no other versions do.

Second, the American first represents a new event in American history and culture. With it, something new was added to our personal heritage. Even if the English or Canadian edition appeared previously, the American edition seems more intimate because it was produced by *our* countrymen and predecessors. Thus American collectors—call them sentimentalists if you will—prefer and are ready to pay, if they can, for the *native* first rather than *the* first. As John Carter points out in *ABC for Book Collectors*, keen collectors want both, but, given a chance, they throw logic to the wind and opt for the American book.[6] (In this way they are no worse than the French, who deem an *édition originale* as the first authorized edition published *in France*.) What *we* want is a piece of our own history, and the American first gives it to us.

Third, and possibly most important, is the fact that the first *is* a first, and the first of *anything* especially enchants us. The first is an "original." All that follows is an imitation or modification. At this point, mythologists will point to that most universal of all myths, the myth of creation: the beginning of a new year, the start of a new day, the birth of a child or horse or goat. There is nothing like a beginning to quicken the human spirit. To hold a beginning in one's hands, then, is to associate oneself with its uniqueness and its promise.

All of this, I realize, can be pushed too far, but I believe that the attraction of the first states goes beyond the usual tangibles, that it is dependent in no small part on the irresistible appeal of firstness and, in Mark Twain's case, on the aura of something quintessentially American. There is an undeniable mystique about these early states that prompts otherwise sane and frugal persons to deliver up prodigious sums of money to obtain them.

It's just as well Mark Twain knows nothing about all this. Since he isn't cut in, he'd be sure that he is being swindled again.

Allison R. Ensor

"Norman Rockwell Sentimentality"

The Rockwell Illustrations for
Tom Sawyer and *Huckleberry Finn*

In his introduction to Alan Gribben's monumental *Mark Twain's Library: A Reconstruction,* Henry Nash Smith decries the "overpowering Norman Rockwell sentimentality" which has "enveloped" the image of Mark Twain and his writings in the mind of the American public and has obscured the true nature of the man and his works.[1] I presume that Professor Smith's reference to the popular illustrator was intended to suggest the fact that Norman Rockwell is well known for having depicted familiar, nostalgic, mildly humorous or mildly touching scenes from everyday life, especially that of the small town or of America's past. Though Rockwell has been widely admired by the public, that admiration has been frequently regarded by critics as another example of the debased taste of the average middle-class, middle-aged American. Rockwell is perhaps the Lawrence Welk of the world of art—or should we say, to come closer to our own discipline, the Edgar A. Guest, the James Whitcomb Riley of art. On the other hand, in an introduction in *Rockwell on Rockwell,* Alden Hatch calls him "a sort of pictorial Mark Twain."[2] This, I submit, strongly suggests that Hatch possessed just the sentimentalized picture of Twain and his writings that Henry Nash Smith was complaining about.

Smith was certainly aware of the one direct link between Clemens and Rockwell. In the 1930s the latter prepared sixteen full-page color illustrations and ninety-one black-and-white drawings

15

for special editions of *The Adventures of Tom Sawyer* and *Adventures of Huckleberry Finn*. I propose to examine the sixteen principal illustrations to see how accurately they have depicted the novels and whether they have helped produce the sentimentalized image of Tom and Huck and their adventures. The smaller black-and-white illustrations—usually appearing on the first page of each new chapter—are not as important and have been reproduced only rarely. For the most part, they depict objects rather than characters or scenes.

In 1935, the centennial year of the birth of Samuel L. Clemens, George Macy, of the Heritage Press in New York, was seeking an illustrator for new editions of *Tom Sawyer* and *Huckleberry Finn*. Outstanding illustrators had worked on other Mark Twain books— N. C. Wyeth did six color illustrations for *The Mysterious Stranger* in 1916, and Howard Pyle illustrated *Saint Joan of Arc* in 1919— but no one, it seemed, had properly done *Tom* and *Huck,* though there *had* been illustrated versions. The first American editions contained many black-and-white drawings by True Williams and E. W. Kemble. Some later editions had perhaps one color illustration—the frontispiece—and then a number of black-and-white pictures. George Macy wanted something more: several color illustrations for each book, plus a number of black-and-white drawings, all catching the spirit of the well-known and well-loved books.

It is hardly surprising that Macy turned to Norman Rockwell to illustrate the new editions. Though many Rockwell pictures that are now familiar to us had not been drawn by that time, he had been doing *Saturday Evening Post* covers for twenty years and had amply demonstrated his mastery at depicting the American scene and, especially, the "American boy." As a recent advertisement for *A Rockwell Portrait* has it, he "uniquely captured the joyous spirit of a bygone America." Who better to draw the scenes that generations of American readers had loved so well? For fifteen years Rockwell had declined offers to illustrate *Tom Sawyer;* now, at last, the most American of illustrators was about to illustrate the most American works of the most American of writers.

At least two major accounts of Rockwell's experiences in producing the illustrations for these volumes appeared during his lifetime. The earlier, by Arthur Guptill, was published in 1946 in his *Norman Rockwell, Illustrator.*[3] The second appeared in 1960 in *My*

Adventures as an Illustrator,[4] ostensibly by Rockwell himself, though really "as told to Thomas Rockwell." It is on these two accounts that I have relied for some of the information which follows.

"Thrilled" by the assignment, Rockwell prepared himself for this task by reading *Tom* and *Huck* and by examining some of the work by previous illustrators. He does not mention names, but this almost surely included the drawings in the first editions. He says that he recognized at once that certain scenes must be pictured—above all, apparently, the whitewashing of the fence. (As a matter of fact, this scene had been drawn by N. C. Wyeth for the dust jacket of a 1931 edition of *Tom Sawyer.*) He also knew that the color plates had to be spread out more or less evenly through the books. They did not have to depict scenes related to the adjacent pages, but it was necessary that the various parts of the novels be represented.

Rockwell was surprised, we are told, to find that no previous illustrator of *Tom* and *Huck* had visited Hannibal, Missouri, Clemens' home and the scene of all of *Tom* and part of *Huck*. This lack of acquaintance with the area was especially true of E. W. Kemble, who had never been in the South at all and had used a New York boy as the model not only for Huck but for every character in the book, black or white, male or female.[5] Rockwell set about changing the previous neglect of Hannibal by visiting the town to "get authentic details." It did not take long to discover how accurately the books had depicted the locale: "And not just the general character of the town but the actual houses, streets, countryside. . . . Almost every physical detail in the books was actual fact, remembered by Twain from his boyhood."[6]

In connection with illustrating a biography of Louisa May Alcott, Rockwell remarked, "If I have an illustration to do in a special setting, I always try to get the feel of the place"[7]—and Hannibal was no exception. One biographer reports that "he talked to inhabitants young and old, he jotted down hundreds of impressions."[8] Sometimes they told him odd things, as when an old judge revealed that "Sam Clemens was really a sickly, sensitive boy, so what he put into his stories were the things he would have done had he been stronger—things that he no doubt dreamed of doing." Rockwell seems to have accepted this reminiscence, for he comments, "If he had actually done those things, possibly he would have been such an extrovert that he could not have written about them."[9] Rockwell then summed up his overall view of the town's importance for the author:

> I have a feeling . . . that if Mark Twain had not been brought up in Hannibal, these stories could not have happened: the place has everything! It's on the Mississippi; it's got the cave, the bluffs, the island, just as they were described in the book; it possesses all the romance of an old-time river town . . . you soon have the feeling that you are living right in these stories; that shows how well they were written.[10]

Besides the physical landscape, Rockwell was impressed by the people, and particularly by "the hats and jackets and pants which the farmers wore around Hannibal." So diligently did he collect old clothes from the inhabitants that word spread to the surrounding area that a "crazy man in Hannibal [was] buying old clothes for high prices."[11]

Rockwell returned to New Rochelle, New York, and began painting his illustrations, for he had done only sketching in Hannibal. With the actual clothes and the images of Hannibal in his mind and notebooks, he worked rapidly. "The illustrations," he later said, with singular appropriateness, "glided along like a raft on the Mississippi in flood."[12] They appeared in the Heritage Press editions of 1936 and 1940, and the originals were given to the Mark Twain Museum in Hannibal, where they are at present on display.

I propose now to examine Rockwell's sixteen full-color illustrations to see what they depict and what they do not depict of the action in the two novels.

The first illustration (fig. 1), the frontispiece for *Tom Sawyer,* is the most famous: Tom whitewashing the fence. It is almost surely the illustration most familiar to the American public, especially since it was used on an 8-cent stamp in 1972. The fence and the part of the house that can be seen (to the left) closely resemble the Clemens house and fence seen by tourists in Hannibal today. The other boy in the picture is not Huck but Ben Rogers, the first of the innocents slaughtered by Tom's knowledge of psychology. The apple he holds is soon to be Tom's.

1. Tom Sawyer whitewashing the fence.

Rockwell's version of the fence, incidentally, is somewhat higher than the version in the first edition, though not as high as that envisioned by other illustrators. The fence has given illustrators trouble because of uncertainty as to the age (and consequently the height) of Tom and how literally one should take the narrator's statement about "thirty yards of board fence nine feet high."[13] Some suppose that this merely represents how high the fence *looked* to Tom that Saturday morning when Aunt Polly put him to work on it. (It is clear that some statements in the novel are subjective, as when we are told that Huck, in response to Tom's urging that he run for his life, "was making thirty or forty miles an hour."[14]) The manuscript shows that the original height of the fence was four feet, before Twain altered it to nine.[15] It is also worth noticing that the planks of Rockwell's fence are vertical, as they are in Hannibal today, though the novel's reference to "the topmost plank" and the streak of whitewash on the ground would indicate that True Williams was correct in showing the planks as horizontal.

A second color illustration shows Tom in church, occupied with nonreligious matters: the dog is investigating a pinchbug which it will soon be all too ready to get rid of. The dog Rockwell has pictured is not a "poodle," as that word is usually understood now (it does not have thick, curly hair), and all indications are that this is an Episcopal church, rather than the Presbyterian church that Tom attended, for the occupants of the pew, Tom included, appear to be kneeling for prayer. Rockwell is supposed to have visited the church attended by the Clemens family in Hannibal,[16] but somehow the kneeling pads and what look like prayer books constitute a false note in the picture. Furthermore, the text states that the congregation stood for prayer (rather than kneeled), and the poodle-and-pinchbug incident occurs during the sermon instead of during the prayer. Thus Rockwell appears not to have followed the novel as closely here as he usually does. Even the window does not seem right: what appear to be green venetian blinds do not fit Twain's reference to the "open window and the seductive outside summer scenes," the reason for Tom's having been placed next to the aisle.

A third illustration (fig. 2) has Tom, with a slate under his arm (since he is on his way to school), being shown a dead cat by Huck Finn. (They will take the cat—a sure cure for warts when properly used—to the graveyard that night.) It may be interesting to com-

2. Huck showing Tom the dead cat.

pare Rockwell's visualization of Huck with the fairly full description Mark Twain gives at this point:

> Huckleberry was always dressed in the cast-off clothes of full-grown men, and they were in perennial bloom and fluttering with rags. His hat was a vast ruin with a wide crescent lopped out of its brim; his coat, when he wore one, hung nearly to his heels and had the rearward buttons far down the back; but one suspender supported his trousers; the seat of the trousers bagged low and contained nothing; the fringed legs dragged in the dirt when not rolled up.[17]

In Rockwell's picture Huck is not wearing a coat and his vest keeps us from seeing whether he is wearing suspenders, though Tom is. The trouser legs must be rolled up, since they lack several inches of touching the ground. One would scarcely say that the clothes of Rockwell's Huck are in bloom with rags, though one bright red rag is to be seen. Otherwise, Huck's clothes and hat appear pretty much as Twain describes them.

The consequence of Tom's admission to the schoolmaster that he had "stopped to talk with Huckleberry Finn" is shown in illustration number four (fig. 3), as Tom gets what once was known as a "whuppin." At least four broken switches lie on the floor; the master is using number five. The girls, presumably including Becky Thatcher (perhaps she is the one on the front row), seem rather sad and sympathetic; at least one of the boys—probably Alfred Temple—appears rather pleased. Rockwell comments that "it was fun picturing the girls so apprehensive and the boys so full of glee."[18] The illustration bears an interesting resemblance to an earlier one by Rockwell, done as an advertisement for a product whose name became a pun in the caption: "Socks."[19]

No whipping was going to prevent Tom from having further association with Huck, and in illustration number five we see him slipping out for a meeting with him. They will shortly be on their way to the cemetery, carrying the dead cat we saw in illustration three. Tom is acting like a cat himself at the moment, meowing as he comes down the drainpipe before crawling across the woodshed roof and dropping to the ground, a stunt that Rockwell himself tried while in Hannibal. Examination of the rear of the Clemens house verifies Rockwell's claim that he "was able to show exact win-

3. Tom gets a whipping.

dow, the very drainpipe and the woodshed" as they presently exist,
if not, as he claims, "just as the author had described them."[20]

I am not entirely convinced, however, that Rockwell has properly depicted Tom's method of leaving his house. The novel says:

> He was dressed and out of the window and creeping along the roof of
> the "ell" on all fours. He "meow'd" with caution once or twice, as he
> went; then jumped to the roof of the woodshed and thence to the
> ground.[21]

Here and elsewhere, one sometimes gets the impression that
Rockwell was more faithful to Hannibal than to Mark Twain.[22]

So far nothing has been seen of Tom's watchful guardian, Aunt
Polly. Her one appearance comes in illustration number six as she
administers a dose of "Pain-Killer" to an obviously miserable Tom.
Peter, the cat, looks on with interest, a nice touch in which Rockwell anticipates a later scene he did not draw: Tom's sharing the
pain killer with the cat, with dramatic results. A slightly different
version of this picture is sometimes reproduced with the title
"Spring Tonic"; it appeared on the cover of the *Saturday Evening
Post* for 30 May 1936. Rockwell described the scene as "really authentic because it is Aunt Polly's living room just as it is still
preserved."[23]

The seventh color illustration depicts Tom, Huck, and Joe
Harper on Jackson's Island (fig. 4) very much alive, though all the
village believes they have been drowned. At this particular moment, two of the would-be pirates may wish they *were* dead,
for Tom and Joe have had their first try at smoking and the experiment has not gone well. Their discarded pipes lie on the ground.
Huck, in the center, is perfectly comfortable, for he is accustomed
to such vices.

Incidentally, on one page in *Norman Rockwell, Illustrator* a
"full-size detail" of Huck is shown, but the subject is identified as
Tom.[24] This is not the only error, either: on a nearby page we hear
of the "switching scene from *Huckleberry Finn*."[25] The writer
seems rather uncertain of the facts of the novel whose illustrations
he is describing. Many Americans, of course, have Tom and Huck
so closely linked in their mind that they cannot separate one from
the other. Even Ernest Hemingway wrote of Jim's being stolen

4. Tom and Huck and Joe on Jackson's Island.

"from the boys,"[26] though Tom was not on the scene and had not been for many chapters.

There seems to be general agreement that the final illustration for *Tom Sawyer* is the poorest, though it has one of the most interesting stories behind it. None of the various volumes of Rockwell illustrations I have seen reproduces this drawing of Tom and Becky in the cave, as Becky cries, "Tom, Tom, we're lost!"

Rockwell was proud of the fact that he alone of the novel's illustrators had properly depicted the cave. During his stay in Hannibal he spent an hour alone in what is now called the Mark Twain Cave. "I discovered," he wrote, "that all the other illustrators had been wrong. They'd painted the cave with stalactites hanging from the roof and sides. It wasn't like that. The rock formation was all horizontal, jutting ledges piled one on top of the other."[27] A look at True Williams' drawing in the first edition will show the error Rockwell was concerned about. It should be noted, though, that Mark Twain specifically mentions stalactites and stalagmites in the cave.[28]

In *Norman Rockwell, Illustrator*, Arthur Guptill tells a dramatic story of Rockwell's experience in the cave. Two murders had just been committed in St. Louis, he says, and the killers were known to be headed for Hannibal. Rockwell's guide took him into the cave and left him alone with a light, because the man's wife was so afraid of the murderers that she could not stand to be left alone. Rockwell's acetylene light went out, leaving him in just the sort of darkness that threatened to envelop Tom and Becky. He waited two and a half hours, fearful that the murderers might have reached Hannibal and might have chosen that very cave as a hiding place. Guptill concludes:

> Suddenly a wavering light appeared in the distance, then drew nearer, eerily illuminating the grotesque forms of that strange interior. Could it be the murderers approaching? His heart quickened. But his fears soon proved to be unfounded—it was only his guide come to conduct him back to the village.[29]

A fine story, indeed—but those who read *My Adventures as an Illustrator*, published some fourteen years later, will learn that the "murderers" were merely bank robbers (though there *was* a rumor that they were hiding in the cave) and that the guide's wife required his presence not because she was afraid but because she was in the late stages of pregnancy. Finally, there is no indication that Rockwell's light went out, though certainly he was scared:

> Something brushed my ear and squeaked. I jumped up, almost knocking over the lamp. There was a low clatter of rocks down one of the tunnels. Sounded like somebody creeping up. . . . The lamp flame wavered. Shadows flickered on the walls. There was a splash of water down a tunnel to the right, a rattle of stones in one behind me.
>
> Well, by the time that guide returned I had all the material I wanted for the picture of Tom and Becky lost in the cave. A surplus, in fact. I was overflowing with it. So loaded down with it that my knees were trembling.[30]

Now that we have seen what Rockwell did with eight color illustrations, I would like to consider what he did *not* do. For one thing, the river never appears, though it is certainly one of the most prominent features of the town, and a number of adventures involve the river. Rockwell mentions sketching the Mississippi "at dawn and noon and dusk,"[31] but it doesn't turn up anywhere in the illustrations.

Second, Rockwell avoided crowd scenes, usually placing one to three people in his pictures. The one exception is the schoolroom scene, when Tom gets his whipping for having stopped to talk with Huck. (There are, of course, some fine crowd scenes in the novel: the trial of Muff Potter, the appearance of the supposedly drowned boys at their own funeral, the gathering of townspeople at the Widow Douglas' house.)

Third, and most important, is almost complete avoidance of anything frightening or horrible. The one major character who never appears in the illustrations is Injun Joe. Unpictured are his killing of Dr. Robinson in the graveyard; his escape from the courtroom, where Tom has revealed the truth about the murder; his climbing the stairs of the haunted house to find whether anyone is hiding there; his approach to the Widow's house to take revenge on her. With the exception of Tom and Becky in the cave, the terrifying, frightening experiences of the novel are all left out, just as they

have disappeared from the memories of many Americans, who recall from the book only a playful summer's day outing on Cardiff
Hill. (The hill, too, is missing from the illustrations, by the way.)

It might also be said that some of the happiest moments are not
shown either, such as the former pirates' reception at the village
church, when the narrator tells us that Tom "confessed in his heart
that this was the proudest moment of his life," or the scene at the
end, where Tom and Huck reveal to the startled onlookers the gold
they have found in the cave.

With this precedent established, we turn to Rockwell's illustrations for *Huckleberry Finn*. The frontispiece shows Huck's return to his room at the Widow's (fig. 5), to find Pap there waiting
for him—probably the most sinister, most uncomfortable moment
Rockwell depicts in this novel. This is Huck's version of Pap's
appearance:

> He was most fifty, and he looked it. His hair was long and tangled
> and greasy, and hung down, and you could see his eyes shining
> through like he was behind vines. It was all black, no gray; so was his
> long, mixed-up whiskers. There warn't no color in his face, where
> his face showed; it was white; not like another man's white, but a
> white to make a body sick, a white to make a body's flesh crawl—a
> tree-toad white, a fish-belly white. As for his clothes—just rags, that
> was all. He had one ankle resting on 'tother knee; the boot on that
> foot was busted, and two of his toes stuck through, and he worked
> them now and then. His hat was laying on the floor; an old black
> slouch with the top caved in, like a lid.[32]

Rockwell picked up such details as the toes sticking out the ends
of the boots and the hat on the floor, though he less successfully
shows Pap's hair, which appears brown, rather than black, and does
not obscure his face as much as the novel calls for. Too, the special
whiteness of Pap's skin is considerably more vivid in Huck's description than in the picture. One may also note that though Pap's
legs are crossed, he is not resting an ankle on the other knee: the
position is more knee-on-knee.

An earlier moment is shown in the second illustration, as Miss
Watson prays with Huck in the closet (because the New Testament
says that one should enter into his closet to pray).[33] A cat looks on,
somewhat in the manner of Peter eyeing the administration of the

5. Pap waiting for Huck in his room.

pain killer, though this time there is no reason for the presence of the cat.

For all his importance in the novel, Jim turns up in only two of the eight illustrations. In the third illustration, he displays an aspect of his superstition as he listens to his hair-ball oracle (fig. 6), which advises Huck to keep away from water—though he spends much of the rest of the novel on the river.

In illustration four, Huck is in disguise as Sarah Williams or Mary Williams (he's not sure which), and Mrs. Judith Loftus is watching with suspicion as he threads a needle in a way a girl would not (fig. 7). "My hands shook," reads the caption, "and I was making a bad job of it." Huck is wearing one of the calico gowns he and Jim had found in a house which floated by. Rockwell's concealment of Huck's face is accurate, for he says: "I put on the sunbonnet and tied it under my chin, and then for a body to look in and see my face was like looking down a joint of stove-pipe."[34]

The King and the Duke appear in the next two illustrations. The first is notable as the sole color picture in either novel that shows the Mississippi River—and even here it is a very small part of the scene (fig. 8). This is the most crowded picture, with Huck, Jim, the King, and the Duke. (Jim, incidentally, looks somewhat younger than in the illustration with the hair-ball oracle.) The moment shown is when the old man reveals his supposed identity, "Your eyes is lookin' at this very moment on the pore disappeared Dauphin, Looy the Seventeen," and it is interesting to compare Rockwell's version with Huck's description of the King:

> One of these fellows was about seventy, or upwards, and had a bald head and very gray whiskers. He had an old battered-up slouch hat on, and a greasy blue woolen shirt, and ragged old blue jeans britches stuffed into his boot tops, and home-knit galluses—no, he only had one. He had an old long-tailed blue jeans coat with slick brass buttons, flung over his arm.[35]

Of the Duke, Huck says only that he was "about thirty and dressed about as ornery."

Obviously, a few liberties have been taken: Rockwell's King has more hair, for one thing, and the one gallus of the King has been transferred to the Duke—though other details have been somewhat faithfully reproduced.

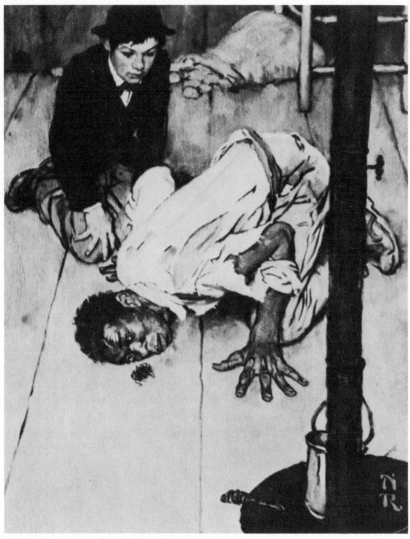

6. Jim listening to hair-ball oracle.

7. Huck disguised as Sarah/Mary Williams.

8. First illustration of the King and the Duke, showing the Mississippi River.

The King and the Duke have their second picture all to themselves, though the text indicates that the room was full of people. The coffin of their supposed brother, Peter Wilks, rests across two chairs in the background, not "in the corner," as Huck says. A flower, which seems to have dropped from the floral decoration on the coffin, fills a space taken by cats in two previous pictures we have discussed. (Another link in Rockwell's work is that the green blinds resemble those in the church where Tom Sawyer became fascinated with the dog and the pinchbug.) The King and the Duke are putting on a show of mourning at this point, which Huck describes thus: "They put their arms around each other's necks, and hung their chins over each other's shoulders; and then for three minutes, or maybe four, I never see two men leak the way they done."[36] Rockwell has depicted the scene accurately, though he has eliminated the audience, which is large enough for Huck to call "the crowd."

Although they do not appear in it, the doings of the King and the Duke lead to the situation in the next-to-last illustration. A very dressed up Huck is in serious conversation with Mary Jane Wilks, oldest of the children in the family the King and the Duke are trying to swindle out of the dead Peter's legacy. The open trunk is being packed by Mary Jane for what she believes will be a journey to England with her "uncles." She is disillusioned, though, as Huck says, "Miss Mary Jane, you can't abear to see people in trouble, and *I* can't—most always,"[37] and proceeds to reveal the truth about his companions.

In defense of Huck's fancy clothes, one may point out that he is supposed to be an English boy, valet to the Wilks brothers, and Huck has reported that "we had all bought store clothes where we stopped last." Actually, we never see Huck looking as grubby as such a boy probably would have been, and few illustrators have been able to do much with Huck's statement that, while on the river, he and Jim went naked a good part of the time.[38]

As in the Heritage Press edition of *Tom Sawyer*, the last picture proved to be one of the least successful, as it seems not to have been reproduced in any of the collections of Rockwell's work. Of all the happenings at the Phelps farm which have so dismayed readers and critics, Rockwell chose a somewhat humorous moment which does not involve Huck, Jim, or the newly arrived Tom: Aunt

Sally Phelps being menaced—so she thinks—by one of the snakes which had been intended as a companion for the imprisoned Jim. The boys who are looking on are not Tom and Huck, but the Phelps children.

In *Huckleberry Finn* as in *Tom Sawyer,* then, Rockwell smoothed over the harsher, darker pages of the novel and emphasized the humorous and the light hearted. The Heritage Club was correct in advising its members that the illustrations "are certain to tickle your fancy as well as your ribs."[39] Rockwell's passion for realism, so apparent in many of his statements about both Twain's writing and his own illustrations for the Twain volumes, did not extend so far as to produce entirely faithful renderings of the novels. Nothing is seen of the Grangerford-Shepherdson feud, of the shooting of Boggs by Colonel Sherburn, of Jim Turner menaced by the men aboard the *Walter Scott,* or of Jim shut up in the cabin at the Phelps place. The novel that Rockwell depicted in his illustrations is something less than the novel Mark Twain wrote, though it may be close to the public image of that novel. What Rockwell fails to show is in many cases precisely what has disappeared from the collective American memory of these books: those moments when the darker side of human nature manifests itself in a way that is frightening and profoundly disturbing.

It is difficult to say to what extent the public image of Tom and Huck and their adventures is based on the Rockwell illustrations. The books in which these pictures originally appeared are still being offered to members of the Heritage Club.[40] Most libraries and bookstores have a number of volumes on Norman Rockwell and his art, and these frequently include several of the *Tom* and *Huck* illustrations. *The Norman Rockwell Album* and *Norman Rockwell's America,* for example, each has eight; six appear in *Norman Rockwell, Illustrator.* Furthermore, slides have been made of all the *Tom Sawyer* illustrations, and these may be purchased in Hannibal by the many tourists who browse through the Becky Thatcher Book Shop. As has been noted, the widest distribution of any Rockwell drawing occurred when the Postal Service chose the whitewashing scene for a 1972 stamp.

It seems reasonable to assume that the Rockwell illustrations have contributed significantly toward creating an image of Tom

and Huck in the minds of the American public, that they are, as
we read in Alden Hatch's introductory sketch in *Rockwell on
Rockwell*, "the definitive visualizations of Mark Twain's immortal
pair."[41] The Heritage Club was quite explicit in its statement to its
members: "After you have looked upon Norman Rockwell's illustrations for *Tom Sawyer*, you will never again think of Mark Twain's
book without thinking of these illustrations."[42]

They have, no doubt, given pleasure to many. One can only
regret that, by their narrow focus, they have masked the incisive
satire of *Huckleberry Finn* and those darker, more terrifying moments in *Tom Sawyer*. The "Norman Rockwell sentimentality," la-
mented by Henry Nash Smith, has surely been furthered by the
work of Rockwell himself.

TWAIN

MYTHOLOGIZES

TWAIN

Alan Gribben

Autobiography
as Property

Mark Twain and His Legend

When "Mark Twain" had lived a full lifetime of seventy-one years—
after his creator died at the age of seventy-four in 1910—a group of
scholars convened in Alabama to discuss this "mythologizing" phenomenon. A legend had survived the man who actually inhabited
nineteenth-century America, imbuing him with dimensions and
attributes of a folk-hero figure of magnificent accomplishments and
incredible adventures. Inevitably, the central question at this academic symposium became: What was the extent of Samuel Clemens' participation in that myth-making process, and how much resulted from our subsequent embellishments, the generous homage
paid by readers and an obliging public to one of our authors of au-
thentically innovative prose? For any student of biography must
concede that the notion of posterity obsessed Clemens more than
it gripped most of his contemporaries, so much so that he virtually
willed the creation of his posthumous legend. However, the historical facts also reveal that those who lived after Clemens' death
helped gild his habitual mask until it became the artifact ultimately
adopted as an American icon.

The possibility that one day the participants at a national confer-
ence might pay tribute to his skillfully designed persona, Mark
Twain, by suggesting that there was even a likelihood of its charismatic qualities eclipsing the achievements of his literary works,
masterful as they are, would not have astonished Clemens during

39

the final decade of his life. Such an acknowledgment most assuredly would have gratified him. He had wanted, if possible, to ensure something more grandiose than the probability that he would merely be remembered in future ages; he craved a guarantee that his name and triumphs would be catalogued among the major features of American cultural and literary history. Accordingly, he took steps during his career to promote his increasingly popular image and to etch it indelibly in the glass door that was swinging open toward our twentieth century.

The efficaciousness of his program is almost incalculable. Is there any other writer whose persona is so well known in a combination of guises: Missouri boy, steamboat pilot, Western prospector, middle-aged traveler, speaker, novelist, old man railing against infirmity and diseases and man's asininity? In comparison with Clemens' river days, for example, Jack London's exciting Oakland–San Francisco oyster-bed pirating, though a potentially intriguing series of youthful escapades, is only as minimally familiar as his novels and short stories.

Few if any American writers and public officials have inspired such a variety of memorials, monuments, restored residences, large-scale manuscript exhibitions, one-man impersonation shows, and catalogues of their libraries. Longfellow, for instance, despite his bardic status at midcentury in Clemens' lifetime, has suffered diminished awe, to the point of little respect. Whitman has fared far better, but he has never become so much larger than the historical record of his biography and writings, nor has Melville risen above sea voyages and the whaling motif, nor Emily Dickinson the disadvantages of her reputation as a recluse who played private word games. Possibly only Abraham Lincoln, who retained the prestige of his office and the tragic aura of the war he directed, merits comparison. General Ulysses S. Grant, a mythic commander of military forces, has gradually undergone a deflation matching public attitudes toward his once-revered tomb. Perhaps, one day, Edith Wharton's knowledge of New York society will reach mythic proportions, but there is no sign of this development. A less literary figure, Will Rogers, has come closer as the apotheosis of ranch life in Oklahoma and of the early Hollywood era. F. Scott Fitzgerald still seems to represent the weaknesses, rather than the strengths, of the Jazz Age. The white-haired Robert Frost earned a degree of affection approaching, but not matching, the esteem Twain enjoys. Ernest Hemingway alone, perhaps, with his boxing, big-game hunting in Africa, deep-sea fishing, and coverage of European battlefronts, has succeeded in transmitting his lusty persona at a level above any possible existence, although the *machismo* of his mask is currently out of fashion. Norman Mailer has of course presented us with exercises in the deliberately obnoxious flaunting of ego and license, but it is too early to predict whether the American public will take such behavior to its heart.

Clemens led the way in modern-day "image making," aided by advances in technology and mass communications. Consequently, the transmission of Twain's legend has taken place less by word of mouth, as former legends survived incrementally from generation to generation, than by Twain's printed books (including his lectures and autobiographical dictations), by Albert Bigelow Paine's authoritative biography and William Dean Howells' *My Mark Twain* and by subsequent biographers, and recently by college instruction, films (including a ninety-second reel made at Stormfield), recordings (though nothing of Clemens' actual voice appears to be extant), and television dramas.

The trappings of a legend afloat in a commercial, urban society are awesome. In the case of Mark Twain, these include a "birthplace shrine" and a boyhood home that has been repainted *gratis* to advertise a line of paint supposedly covering "Great American Homes." There have been liquor and cigar advertisements featuring Mark Twain's likeness, as well as banks that use his name and portrait on their checks, and airlines that show him riding first class. Numerous rare-book and manuscript collectors specialize in Mark Twain items. State parks are named after Mark Twain. A civic group has restored the mansion he built in Hartford in 1874. A well-publicized jumping frog contest is sponsored annually in Calaveras County. Twain has been honored with a postage stamp. The Mississippi River towns of Hannibal, Keokuk, Muscatine, St. Louis, and New Orleans take civic pride in his associations with their environs. Eminent radio artists have recorded readings of his stories. Hal Holbrook has engendered a host of imitators who mimic *him* as well as his chief subject. A scholarly publishing project in Berkeley is editing his writings, published and unpublished. Public and commercial television networks have presented dramas based on his life and works. The film industry has undertaken numerous projects related to Twain. His quips appear regularly in the editorial columns of daily newspapers, and have been collected conveniently in a dictionary of quotations. Scarcely any other authors are as widely taught and written' about at universities and colleges in disciplines as diverse as social history and American literature.

One of the few French philosophers whom Twain truly respected was responsible for the familiar quip, "If God did not exist, it would be necessary to invent him." A humbler variation on Voltaire's theme could apply here: If the historical figure of Mark Twain had never been born in Missouri, had never achieved his international fame, and never left behind his legend as a cultural symbol, would it not have been necessary for the United States to discover a comparable author? More to the point, are we not continually reinventing and refining his image to meet our contemporary needs and anxieties about our national character and the history of our literature? For as the complicated story of Samuel Clemens became the simplified legend of Mark Twain, it also formed the psychohistory of an age in America.

His unparalleled success can partly be gauged by the reluctance of the popular mind nowadays to accept Samuel Clemens' physical measurements: his diminutive height and weight have gained robustness with each decade, along with his literary reputation. A more hilarious evolution can be witnessed in our electronic-media equivalent of the oral tradition, the made-for-television movie, which produced in 1977 an absurdity titled *The Incredible Rocky Mountain Race,* starring Chris Connelly as young Mark Twain and Forrest Tucker as Mike Fink. In this travesty of folklore and history, the reporter Twain and the river boatman Fink race each other from Missouri to California, a competition encouraged by the townspeople of St. Joseph (!), Missouri, who are eager to rid themselves of two cantankerous frontiersmen. The winner is to be declared "King of the West." The entertainment specialists responsible for contriving such fabrications evidently sense that the outlines of Twain's actual biographical existence are loosening, that he can be conveniently utilized in any situation involving settings in the American Far West. In their story, Twain encounters Jim Bridger and William F. Cody along the route of his race, and Twain proves to be nearly as much a roughneck, daredevil, and talltalker as the bragging Mike Fink. For the popular imagination, it would seem, Twain represents almost anything favorable or amusing about our heritage.

The fact is, Mark Twain is one of the threads of richest hue in our tapestry of national history. Therefore, like Shaw, Dickens, Johnson, or Shakespeare, he can be cited in many situations and quoted on diverse occasions. He represents for writers and orators the young aspirations of the Western American settlements, the adventure and skill of an era of Mississippi River piloting, the pluck and hardihood of Nevada and California mining, the intrepid endurance of an international traveling correspondent, the determination and talent of the men and women who forged the American Realism movement of literature. Lately he has further become, in our cynical decades of aging national life, the grumpy grandfather of our mounting complaints and obvious foibles. No other person of his time came close to embodying so many of the virtues, idiosyncracies, and failures that his later countrymen would eventually cherish and idealize—not Horace Greeley, not Susan B. Anthony, not Henry Ward Beecher, not Robert Ingersoll, not P. T. Barnum, not Finley Peter Dunne, not Theodore Roosevelt. Often credited with maxims he never invented, he stands alone in our popular affection, and in the growth of his legend. People still inquire of professors of literature about when the *truly* vitriolic Twain manuscripts will finally be published, those scathing indictments his daughter and other suppressors purportedly have held back for fear of the public's horror and outrage. These imagined after-shocks only help the average citizen identify all the more with an intemperate, courageous writer.

On the campus, he remains a favorite of most English and history instructors, flavoring the syllabus with a tangy hint of rebellious, anti-academic subversiveness. For most critics and scholars, Professor Lewis Leary was conjuring up a familiar image in imagining Mark Twain's satisfaction with the first two volumes of his *Notebooks & Journals*, as published in 1975 in Berkeley. "Not since [Twain] was given that gorgeous red robe at the University of Oxford has anything pleased Mark Twain more. He doffs his halo, knocks the ashes from his cigar, and reaches under his star-studded celestial gown for that amphora-jug of whatever ambrosial nectar he has conned some heavenly acquaintance to keep him supplied with to drink their health," Professor Leary speculated in a clever *Sewanee Review* essay.[1] Here are nicely summarized the essential ingredients of the Twain we admire: the flamboyance of his dress and demeanor, including an Oxford robe; the halo, won in spite of his incorrigibly youthful ways on earth; the cigar, smoked in defiance of physicians and Mrs. Aldrich; the secret cache of liquor, savored with a knowing wink; the genial mirthfulness and detached viewpoint regarding the posthumous prying of academic annotators. Also implied, perhaps, is the darker, all-comprehending intellect that broods with us over the limitations of humankind's lifespan and ability.

Professors and the rest of his countrymen are not mistaken in discerning these and other endearing qualities in Twain's personality and career, but the legend that merits study also deserves analysis into its origins. In this endeavor we can trace its sources not only in Twain's life, but also in his writings and those of his contemporaries, particularly William Dean Howells and Albert Bigelow Paine, who, with later biographers, accepted and disseminated Twain's version of events. Slowly, our contemporary biographers have recognized the contradictions and discrepancies in that version, a process culminating in Hamlin Hill's startling disclosures.

If the crucial beginning of these assumptions was Twain's writings themselves, especially his autobiographical narratives, the twentieth-century vehicle was Paine's influential biography. Most Americans would have been surprised by the notion that Mark Twain *needed* an officially authorized biography; his life, after all, had supposedly been encapsulated in his books. Albert Bigelow Paine was allowed, however, to fill in the family and personal details that Twain had passed over in his works for fear of failing to amuse the reader. There was a streak in Paine that responded to celebrities who overcame adversity and arose from early obscurity. His later biography, *Life and Lillian Gish* (1932), published shortly after talking pictures had retired most silent-film stars, traced the rise of the heroine of *Birth of a Nation*. Paine recalls: "I sent a note to Miss Gish, proposing to write of her. I had given up such work as too arduous, but it seemed to me that this might be a happy thing to do—the story of one who had begun humbly, and walked in beauty and humility to achievement, making the world better and lovelier for her coming."[2] Lacking the stylistic vigor and concrete observations of the Mark Twain biography, the Gish book rarely approaches the level of that work of twenty years previous. At the end, Paine extols the "slim-legged little girl, who slept on station benches and telegraph tables, who running across a foot-bridge lost her poor possessions in the swift black water, who from a train or hotel window stared silently into the night" (p. 303).

Precisely what is the legend about Mark Twain that enraptured Albert Bigelow Paine and still infatuates us? That a poor Midwestern boy masters steamboat piloting, then proceeds to write articulately about the scenes and attitudes of nearly every part of his homeland and many regions of England, Europe, and the Middle East—retiring in a magnificent Italian-style villa in the hills of Connecticut, his name to be familiar to his countrymen and foreigners alike for generations to come. This approximates the pattern of Horatio Alger tales, but in Twain's variant the protagonist smiles through tears and succeeds so gloriously that his enemies are devoured by envy. He can do something well. He has won a triumph, learning from setbacks. Whether he has been victimized by a Mexican plug horse or an unscrupulous merchant, he exaggerates his bitterness so ludicrously that we laugh. He boasts outrageously—in *A Tramp Abroad*, of his supposedly hard work in rafting, mountain climbing, hotel visiting. And he never takes too seriously his association with so many famous people of his day. Irreverent humor will triumph effortlessly, he seems to claim, provided that we remember how ridiculous and credulous is the mass of humanity.

Clemens passed his final years shaping and adjusting the image he hoped to leave behind, utilizing each newspaper and magazine interview.[3] When he died, he was mourned by every section of the United States, for he had linked himself with most parts of the nation (except Florida, the Pacific Northwest, and Texas), becoming an American of no particular region, erasing his regionalism rather than emphasizing it. He had stayed long enough to master various new environments, then moved on, moving West (like the imagination of the country), and at last returning East to report and reminisce. He left behind an identity with each region, and the inhabitants thanked him for making their humdrum existence seem novel and amusing. (Twain established more regional identities than Harriet Beecher Stowe, citizen of Ohio, Maine, Connecticut, Florida; George Washington Cable, who combined Louisiana and Massachusetts; John Steinbeck, of California and New York City; Neil Simon, the East Coast, the West Coast, the desert Southwest. Twain had the Mississippi River Valley, from Muscatine to New Orleans; Nevada and California; the city of Buffalo; New England and Hartford; the European continent, especially England, Germany, France, Switzerland, and Austria; New York City; and finally Redding, Connecticut.)

As a result of Clemens' intention to surpass rivals such as Bret Harte in future acclaim as well as present-day sales, and his anxiety about his lack of formal education, he came to value every morsel, every scrap, every particle of his life, placing a mercenary price on each incident and episode as they befell him. His biographical experiences were viewed the same way he had seen men in Nevada and California approach those inert, lucrative mountains: he intended to work them like a paying ore mine; his life was a lode, vein, grubstake, payload, tracer, unpanned claim, bonanza. His determined attitude resembled his literary advice to William Wright, known as Dan De Quille, when the latter was undertaking a book about the Western mines: "I'll show you how to make a man read every one of those sketches, under the stupid impression that they are mere accidental incidents that have dropped in on you unawares in the course of your *narrative*."[4]

Twain's terrific possessiveness about his posthumous image was no more fierce than his proprietary feelings about personal manuscripts and letters. Even the methodical autograph hunter was, in his words, "another phase of human depravity" (New York *Herald*, 20 January 1901). On 19 October 1865, in the famous letter that Clemens wrote to his brother and sister-in-law from San Francisco, he acknowledged that he was yielding to "a 'call' to literature of a low order—i.e., humorous. It is nothing to be proud of, but it is my strongest suit." He added a postscript (futilely, as it proved) that same night: "P. S. You had better shove this in the stove—for . . . I don't want any absurd 'literary remains' & 'unpublished letters of Mark Twain' published after I am planted" (ALS in Mark Twain Project, Berkeley). To Orion Clemens he boasted in 1887: "I have never yet allowed an interviewer or biography-sketcher to get out of me any circumstance of my history which I thought might be worth putting some day into my *auto-biography*. . . . I hate all public mention of my private history, anyway. It is none of the public's business. . . . I have been approached as many as five hundred times on the biographical-sketch lay, but they never got anything that was worth the printing."[5] This point of view was hardly unique to Clemens, of course. One of Clemens' most admired poets, Rudyard Kipling, refused a request to cooperate with a biography of his aunt, Lady Burne-Jones, explaining: "My objection stands, tho' it be a selfish one. I'm too fond of her, and loved her too much in my childhood and youth, to share my feelings with *any* public. This here biography and 'reminiscer' business that is going on nowadays is a bit too near the Higher Cannibalism to please me. Ancestor-worship is all right, but serving them up filleted, or spiced or 'high' (which last is very popular) has put me off."[6]

After a man named Will M. Clemens published *Mark Twain: His Life and Work* in 1892, he had the audacity to write to the celebrated man with whom he shared a name, but no kinship, requesting permission to publish *The Mark Twain Story Book*, "The Homes and Haunts of Mark Twain," and a biographical sketch. Clemens replied wth acerbity on 6 June 1900: "I am sorry to object, but I really must. Such books as you propose are not proper to publish during my lifetime. A man's history *is his own property* until the grave extinguishes his ownership in it. I am strenuously opposed to having books of a biographical character published about me while I am still alive."[7] This sense of his autobiographical details as a form of property infused his attitudes throughout the remainder of his life, and can be detected in the letter he wrote to Henry H. Rogers, seeking legal assistance from his Standard Oil patron: "Here is this troublesome cuss, Will M. Clemens, turning up again. I won't have it. . . . Watch for advertisements of these books . . . so that you can set Wilder or some other brisk lawyer to work squashing them at the right time. . . . [Will] Clemens can't write books— he is a mere maggot who tries to feed on people while they are still alive." Unavailingly, Will Clemens tried to argue the point further: "In no instance have I or would I copy a single line of your copyrighted work. But your public spoken utterances become public property once they are spoken and there is no law against writing truthful facts concerning a man's life. The book is shelved for the moment much to my regret and loss—I can wait" (*MTHHR*, p. 447, n. 2).

Aware that aggravating meddlers like Will Clemens were lurking in the wings, Samuel Clemens faced his dwindling years with concern about what might happen once he was incapacitated, rendered helpless to affect the outcome. At least there was consolation in the fact that he had long promoted his many books as making up the record of his life. One manifestation of this effort, *Mark Twain's Library of Humor* (1888), edited by Clemens in collaboration with William Dean Howells and Charles Hopkins Clark, included a headnote to the first selection from each humorist's writings. Mark Twain's own introduction, printed above "The Notorious Jumping Frog," reads:

> Samuel L. Clemens (Mark Twain) was born at Hannibal, Mo., in 1835, and after serving an apprenticeship to the printing business in his brother's office there, "learned the river," as pilot. . . . His earliest book, "The Innocents Abroad," was the result of his experience and observation as a passenger on the *Quaker City* in her famous cruise to the Holy Land. His succeeding books *continue the story of his own life*, with more or less fullness and exactness. After his return from Palestine, he was for a year in Buffalo, N. Y., but has ever since lived in Hartford, Conn. [p. 1; italics added]

That phrase, "the story of his own life," would become a refrain in the subsequent biographies, films, and literary criticism. Albert Bigelow Paine's *Boy's Life of Mark Twain* (1916) was reissued in 1916 and 1944 as *The Adventures of Mark Twain*, implying the existence of a white-suited, cigar-smoking, aged Tom Sawyer. In 1917 Paine would choose extracts from one book to make another, titled *The Real Tom Sawyer*. All of this presumably inspired Warner Brothers' feature-length film of 1944, *Adventures of Mark Twain*, starring Fredric March, adapted from Harold L. Sherman's play. A decade later, Jerry Allen published *The Adventures of Mark Twain*. Other biographies and memoirs continued this polite, idealized tone: Howells' *My Mark Twain* (1910), Elizabeth Wallace's *Mark Twain and the Happy Island* (1913). Everyone wanted a share in the literary industry that Twain had founded and incorporated. Katy Leary and Mary Lawton produced *A Lifetime with Mark Twain* (1925); Clara Clemens, *My Father, Mark Twain* (1931); Minnie M. Brashear, *Mark Twain: Son of Missouri* (1934); Ivan Benson, *Mark Twain's Western Years* (1938); Cyril Clemens, *Young Sam Clemens* (1942); and DeLancey Ferguson, the most aptly named *Mark Twain: Man and Legend* (1943).

Viewed chronologically, Twain's travel narratives, novels, short stories, sketches, essays, and speeches take up the events of his life in a curious order, skipping from recent episodes to earliest ones, then returning to later incidents, then intermixing them almost capriciously, as though linear time narrative had no validity, making the phases of his life the apparent jumble that both *Mark Twain's Library of Humor* and his autobiographical dictations—two literary productions that he controlled entirely—turned out to be. Clemens and his commentators were correct in noting that the story of his life was in his books, but the order of narration is far from uniform or predictable. "The Turning Point of My Life" (1910), for example, an essay searching for cause-and-effect occurrences in his boyhood, appeared during his final months. Beginning in 1876, however, one feature became consistent: Mark Twain recurrently returned to what Henry Nash Smith has labeled "The Matter of Hannibal," or what in the popular imagination might be called "The Adventures of Mark Twain," after the books and film by that title. As Larzer Ziff has commented, "He . . . visualized his career as an ellipse that would turn and turn again past the town rather than as a steady movement out-ward. . . . Formed by the drowsing river town, Mark Twain held steadily in his career to the community of his adolescence." Though he never went back to Hannibal to live, "he always remained in orbit around its values. . . . [He had] a belief in experience as valuable to the extent that the town recognizes its distinction and admires it."[8]

It is worthwhile to be reminded that Clemens did not arrive at a full appreciation of the appeal of "the story of his own life" all at once, and that he failed to recognize the material that ultimately gave him his greatest fame and furnished the revered aspects of his Mississippi River background, until he was more than forty years of age, and only after other writers—particularly Thomas Bailey Aldrich in *The Story of a Bad Boy* (1869)—had preceded him in various ways and had supplied him with usable examples. In "The Celebrated Jumping Frog" (1865) he recounted a mining-camp experience that presumably happened lately; in *Innocents Abroad* (1869) a voyage from which the correspondent-vandal had just returned; in *Roughing It* (1872) a Far West saga already in danger of losing its credibility; in *The Gilded Age* (1873) a steamboat explosion, a Missouri village, and the Washington scene; in "Old Times" (1875) a cub pilot's narrative of long-past history; at last, in *Tom Sawyer* (1876), the escapades of boys who swam in the Mississippi River before the Civil War.

Though this autobiographical impulse of Mark Twain is a characteristic strain in American literature, nonetheless, current literary criticism regularly berates the attention to Samuel Clemens' personal life that dilutes so many serious interpretations of his writings. Obviously the man and the works can scarcely be separated without tremendous, premeditated effort. Moreover, this notion of synonymity between Twain and his writings is hardly new. A Princeton professor of English observed in 1904:

> The autobiographic element in the work of Mark Twain has often been pointed out, but it is not perhaps generally realized that the interest of his books varies directly in proportion to the presence of this personal element. . . . He is at his best when he is recording his own experiences; and in his happiest vein when he is transfusing them into a work of art, as in his crowning achievements of *Tom Sawyer* and *Huckleberry Finn*. And this is because his life itself has been typically—one might almost say, uniquely—American. . . . We hardly need the author's assurance that most of the adventures in *Tom Sawyer* really occurred, for the story breathes conviction from every page. The scenes in the schoolroom, the Sunday-school, and the village church reproduce for us the atmosphere of the little inland town as persuasively as Mr. Aldrich's *Bad Boy* does that of old New England.[9]

Yet sometimes a single lifetime seemed insufficient to Clemens. He mastered the craft of writing books so adroitly that he could barely reclaim autobiographical materials rapidly enough to keep his machinelike pen in operation. He began to long for a Clemens-clone, or at least a remote-controlled robot recorder. This fantasy first became explicit in his letter (written from Buffalo on 28 November 1870) to his publisher Elisha Bliss: "I have put my greedy hands on the best man in America for my purpose and shall *start him to the diamond fields of South Africa within a fortnight, at my expense.* I shall write a book of his experiences for next spring, . . . and write it just as if I had been through it all myself, but will explain in the preface that this is done merely to give it life and reality. . . . This thing is brim-full of fame and fortune for both author and publisher."[10]

The victim-beneficiary of this scheme was James H. Riley, a veteran of mining camps in California, Mexico, and Central America, whom Clemens had known in Washington, where Riley had become a clerk to several U.S. senators. Clemens persuaded Riley to leave for the diamond fields by promising to pay him $100 a month and his passage to South Africa. Riley could collect up to $5,000 worth of diamonds, but above that amount he must send half the profits to his patron. He was to keep detailed diaries of his months of prospecting and then consent to live in Clemens' house for up to a year, "for, the purpose of your diary is to keep *you* . . . bright and inspire your tongue every morning when you take a seat in my study. You are to talk one or two hours to me every day, and *tell* your story."[11] Clemens liked to joke that Jules Verne had in effect dispatched his doppelgänger to collect adventures in remote, dangerous regions. To Riley he explained: "I should write this book as if *I* went through all these adventures myself—this in order to give it snap and freshness. But would begin the book by saying: 'When Daniel de Foe wanted to know what life on a solitary island was like, and doubted whether he was hardy enough to stand it himself, he sent the ingenious Robinson W. Crusoe; and when I wanted to know all about wild life in the diamond fields and its fascinations, and could not go myself, I sent the ingenious Riley'" (*MTLP*, pp. 48–49). Like Clemens' typesetter venture, this South African pipe dream had some basis in reality: there was a genuine possibility that American readers would have relished a firsthand account of the scramble for precious gems. And whereas Mergenthaler's Linotype invention would eclipse Clemens' typesetting machine, another African exploit began unfolding simultaneously with Clemens' brainstorm about the diamond fields, a journalism stunt destined to place the words "Dr. Livingstone, I presume?" in history books. By a coincidence that points up how unerringly Clemens' hunches anticipated and paralleled events that made other people famous, in the previous year (1869) newspaper editor James Gordon Bennett had secretly commissioned Henry M. Stanley to penetrate central Africa and find David Livingstone as a scoop for the New York *Herald*. Stanley started his expedition on 21 March 1871 and reached Livingstone on 10 November 1871. But Clemens' South Africa enterprise merely illustrated the unpredictability of human affairs: James Riley, who yielded to Clemens' blandishments, became gravely ill before he and Clemens could commence the proposed schedule of dictations, and this defective other self died in 1872.[12] Clemens, grudgingly, had to reimburse the American Publishing Company for $2,000, money optimistically advanced to the ill-fated Riley.

The linchpin of Clemens' interpretation of his life was the series of autobiographical dictations he left behind to forestall unauthorized versions of his legend. He labored on these in earnest during the final six years of his life, especially in 1906 and 1907. From the first, he claimed to have discovered a new freedom of expression in their uncensored, conversational form. On 10 January 1906 Clemens observed, in his Autobiographical Dictation, that "an autobiography that leaves out the little things and enumerates only the big ones is no proper picture of the man's life at all."[13] These minor incidents would constitute what Henry Adams once called a "shield of protection in the grave," a way to "take your own life . . . in order to prevent biographers from taking it in theirs."[14] He could say anything he wished here, Clemens gloated. He could speak of foreign missionary work as "that least excusable of all human trades."[15]

He would have concurred with William Sydney Porter (O. Henry), who declared in 1909 or 1910: "I do not remember ever to have read an autobiography, a biography, or a piece of fiction that told the *truth*. Of course, I have read such stuff as Rousseau and Zola and George Moore; and various memoirs that were supposed to be window panes in their respective breasts; but mostly, all of them were either liars, actors, or poseurs. . . . The trouble about writing the truth has been that the writers . . . were trying either to do a piece of immortal literature, or to shock the public or to please editors. Some of them succeeded in all three, but they did not write the *truth*."[16] Howells had indicated mild skepticism in a well-known letter of 14 February 1904: "I'd like immensely to read your autobiography," he wrote to Clemens. "I fancy you may tell the truth about yourself. But *all* of it? . . . Even *you* won't tell the black heart's-truth. The man who could do it would be famed to the last day the sun shone on."[17]

Assuredly, Clemens' autobiographical dictations are no standard collection of polite character sketches, but their "truth" is scarcely an issue. They form a labyrinthian exploration of his fictionalizing genius, introducing as many foes as friends, less interested in properly recording history than in giving his version of it a liveliness that is impossible either to contravene or to resist. He skimps most on those incidents concerning illustrious personages that received the chief attention in the earlier memoirs of Howells and Andrew D. White and other works he respected—meetings with social lions and celebrated authors—and emphasizes instead the shouted insult of old Tom Nash, the chicanery of publishers and business associates, the random conversation with a passing acquaintance. However, Albert Bigelow Paine noted insightfully: "The things he told of Mrs. Clemens and of Susy were true—marvelously and beautifully true, in spirit and in aspect—and the actual detail of these mattered little in such a record. The rest was history only as *Roughing It* is history, or the *Tramp Abroad;* that is to say, it was fictional history, with fact as a starting-point." "We were watching," wrote Paine of those open-air dicating sessions, "one of the great literary creators of his time in the very process of his architecture."[18]

There were two Mark Twains, as it turned out: the affable St. Petersburg–Tom Sawyerish–Mississippi River cub pilot, and the raging autobiographical dictation curmudgeon who now erupted daily. Perversely, Twain would have it that both impressions should be left behind for later ages to reconcile, if possible. Today it seems as though, in the latter mood, Clemens viewed himself as a potential Émile Zola in those unpopular crusades against Belgian and American imperialism, General Funston, missionaries, and other professions and personalities; he had been much impressed with Zola's "J'Accuse!," which had appeared in a Paris journal in January 1898 while Clemens was living in Vienna.

The reactions of the modern age to Clemens' heresies have been more accommodating than he could have envisioned. Van Wyck Brooks phrased it succinctly in *The Ordeal of Mark Twain:* "He was irritable, but literary men are always supposed to be that; he was old, and old people are often afflicted with doubts about the progress and welfare of mankind; he had a warm and tender heart, an abounding scorn of humbug." [19]

The aging Clemens, contemplating his place in the annals of American literature, culture, and history, had mentioned in a letter of the 1900s to his daughter Clara: "I go out frequently and exhibit my clothes. Howells has dubbed me the 'Whited Sepulchre.' Yes, dear child, I'm a 'recognized immortal genius' and a most dissipated one too." Clara added that her father "was now so generally recognized by everyone on the street or in public places that it was difficult to realize he was only a man of letters. Sometimes he was greeted by applause when he entered a theater or public dining-room." [20]

And yet after 1904 Clemens had no living wife to write a memoir like *Crowding Memories,* as Mrs. Thomas Bailey Aldrich loyally did; his only relative with literary inclinations, Samuel Moffett, drowned in 1908. After 1909, in fact, Clemens had no close relative, except one songstress daughter. Toward the end of his life, Clemens merely had a reliable publisher, Harper and Brothers, which was expertly guided in its decisions by Frederick Duneka; a trustworthy authorized biographer, Albert Bigelow Paine; and, until 1909, a devoted private secretary, Isabel V. Lyon. With these resources Clemens faced the future void. He had tried to establish the so-called "story of his own life" in numerous travel narratives and novels, and he would release selected excerpts from his autobiographical dictations. Then, finally, there would be that (lately discovered) self-justifying, malicious letter Clemens wrote to Howells about Isabel Lyon's character and behavior. He could also benefit from the autobiographical writings of Howells and White and others, such as Benjamin Franklin and Benvenuto Cellini, who had demonstrated methods of prefabricating one's professional reputation and personal memorial. Here were stratagems to keep one from vanishing without residual honor and affection, the fate of talented men like A. D. Richardson and Artemus Ward.

Understandably, Clemens' confidence deserted him at the end.

Clara recalled that, during his final illness, "he appeared skeptical
. . . as to whether the sale of his books would continue for more
than a brief period after his death," and he told Clara he regretted
not leaving behind more money.[21] Only a few months later, in
1911, the executors of the estate dispersed much of his private library at an urgent sale in New York City, as though intending to
capitalize on what could be fleeting fame, but they need not have
rushed. As Justin Kaplan remarks, he bequeathed us "a legendary
life and a dazzling presence, one of the shaping styles of America's
literature and thought, half a dozen of its major books, and . . . in
the end Mark Twain is more imposing than the sum of his work."
Clemens, "a genius at generating publicity, had created Mark
Twain, a public figure recognizable on almost any street in America."[22] Every passing decade further blurs the distinctions between
Samuel L. Clemens and his better-known alter ego. It can now be
recognized that, mixed in with his many books, was another su-
premely self-conscious work of art, Mark Twain's enduring legend.

Henry Nash Smith

Mark Twain, "Funniest Man in the World"[1]

At the turn of the twentieth century, the image evoked by the name Mark Twain was a conspicuous element in American popular culture. During the decade before the writer's death in 1910, commentators in the press asserted that he was the best known among living persons.[2] An image so widely disseminated was bound to undergo distortion because, as a collective representation, it registered the desires and fantasies and, above all, the stereotyped expectations of millions of people.

I should like to inquire into the cultural forces that determined how Mark Twain was perceived during his lifetime by the general public. Of course I cannot hope to do more than sketch the outlines of the subject, which is a vast one, even though I confine my attention mainly to comment published in newspapers, leaving out criticism appearing in books and literary journals. Fortunately, there is no need for me to track down primary sources, since the basic documents have been collected by half a dozen scholars.[3] I have also drawn heavily on the two Ashcroft scrapbooks of clippings from the British press. I have done a little digging in American newspaper files, but not very much, for the materials already available allow one to identify with reasonable confidence the main patterns of attitude and opinion.

The inquiry is complicated by the fact that throughout Mark Twain's career he suffered from ambiguity concerning his role as an

56

artist. Although no one at the time realized it, the root of the difficulty was language. Neither he nor his audiences, whether popular or learned, could accept the possibility that serious literature might employ as its vehicle a written version of vernacular speech. The problem appears clearly, for example, in the discrepancy between James Russell Lowell's theory and practice. His *Biglow Papers*, denouncing the Mexican War in the 1840s and supporting the Union cause in the 1860s, shows a remarkable gift for recording New England rural dialect. Furthermore, in the 75-page introduction to the second series (1867), devoted almost entirely to Yankee speech, he called attention to the expressive power of language that has "its roots in the living generations of men," as contrasted with "a literate dialect [that] grows more and more pedantic and foreign, till it becomes at last as unfitting a vehicle for living thought as monkish Latin." Yet he was unable to put this insight into practice. Two pages earlier he had apologized for using dialect, saying:

> If I put on the cap and bells and made myself one of the court-fools of King Demos, it was less to make his majesty laugh than to win a passage to his royal ears for certain more serious things which I had deeply at heart. I say this because there is no imputation that could be more galling to any man's self-respect than that of being a mere jester.[4]

For exalted occasions, Lowell considered a "literate dialect" appropriate; his most celebrated poem, the Harvard "Commemoration Ode," is strewn with phrases that echo "Lycidas" and *Macbeth*.[5]

Even Lowell's word "jester," evoking a medieval or Renaissance royal court, has a literary flavor. The more common term, "humorist," was undergoing a rapid semantic change in both British and American usage. As late as the 1850s, in lectures delivered in both countries, Thackeray had included among "English Humourists of the Eighteenth Century" Addison, Swift, and even Pope. But by that time a new kind of humor with a strong vernacular flavor, originating in the United States, had gained such popularity on both sides of the Atlantic that the conception of humor as a species of urbane wit was beginning to seem archaic. The American humorists were not merely without pretensions to elegance; they devoted much energy to burlesquing the literary idols of high culture. At the same time, in this country at least, the Man of Letters was being endowed with more and more of the status and functions of a priest or clergyman. A widely shared American attitude is recorded by Rebecca Harding Davis in her account of her first visit to New England in 1862, as an aspiring young writer from the backwoods of West Virginia. Looking back forty years later, she recalled that she considered Emerson "the first of living men," the "modern Moses who had talked with God apart and could interpret Him to us." "When I heard him coming into the parlor at the Wayside," she declared, "my body literally grew stiff and my tongue dry with awe."[6]

The dinner given by H. O. Houghton, publisher of the *Atlantic Monthly*, to commemorate John Greenleaf Whittier's seventieth birthday in 1877, dramatized the institution of the Man of Letters.[7] William Dean Howells, who as editor of the *Atlantic* presided over the ceremony, remarked later that Whittier and the other guests of honor, Emerson, Holmes, and Longfellow, commanded a "species of religious veneration"; and a reporter for the Boston *Advertiser* asserted that the presence of these writers "gave a reverend, almost holy, air to the place." Mark Twain himself, whose contribution to the program was denounced in some quarters as "irreverent," stated in the course of his speech that "we and the world pay loving reverence and homage" to these venerable figures.

The notion of reverence figured routinely in discussions of literature in the 1870s and 1880s. It called to mind an elaborate system of values, not merely esthetic but moral and even basically political, for the assumed dimensions of "high" and "low" were more than just a matter of rhetoric; they involved a distinction between a small upper class, assumed to be cultivated, and a large lower class of the uncultivated. The reactions to Mark Twain's speech at the Whittier dinner revealed that major cultural issues were involved in the literary burlesque, which was a staple of native American humor.

In Mark Twain's little joke he pretended that three tramps invaded a miner's cabin in the Mother Lode country of California and imposed themselves on their involuntary host as Emerson, Holmes, and Longfellow. The element of burlesque consisted mainly in the speaker's use of quotations from the writings of these great Men of Letters, often very amusingly applied to the farcical situation. When the text of the speech was published the next day in the newspapers, it drew objections from as far away as San Francisco. The incident itself was of course trivial but it reveals a dilemma that would baffle Mark Twain throughout the remaining thirty years of his life. Even such critics as Howells, who recognized intimations of greatness in the writer's best work, were obliged to concede that it was an outgrowth of a tradition of backwoods story telling, which was decidedly unliterary.

The usual assumption in this country was that no merger was possible between serious literature and humor. Literature was a part of high culture; and humor, certainly the backwoods variety, was considered irremediably low.[8] Mark Twain, with part of his mind, shared the conventional opinion. In an interesting letter written from San Francisco to his brother in 1865, in which the thirty-year-old newspaperman earnestly discussed his choice of a vocation, he remarked apologetically that he had "a 'call' to literature, of a low order—i.e., humorous. It is nothing to be proud of, but it is my strongest suit."[9] When he went East and began paying court to Olivia Langdon of Elmira, New York, she and her parents were distressed by the fact that the young journalist from California belonged to this immensely popular but disreputable school, which seemed to make irreverence its stock in trade.[10]

Mark Twain had found by experiment that his lecture audiences enjoyed an occasional burst of rhetorical sublimity, and he could produce this kind of thing at will. The San Francisco *Evening Bulletin*, reviewing Clemens' first lecture on the Sandwich Islands in 1866, reported that "from the lecturer's reputation as a humorist, . . . the audience were unprepared for the eloquent description of the volcano . . . their appreciation of which was shown by . . . continued applause."[11] In our day, we can enjoy the anecdotes redolent of "slang" in Mark Twain's early work, and his burlesques of popular novels and plays,[12] but the taste for oratorical eloquence has disappeared and we are disconcerted by his rapid shifts from ridicule of pompous rhetoric to apparently serious use of it. This mixture of high and low styles is even less satisfactory in written than in oral discourse. Mark Twain would struggle for many years, usually in vain, to devise literary forms that would enable him to dispense with it. In his Sandwich Islands lecture, after he had rendered his "word painting" of the eruption of Kilauea, he would sometimes convulse his audience by muttering, "Let someone beat that for harnessing adjectives together."[13] Nevertheless, his impulse to show off his ability to produce conventional literary effects would eventually control the composition of entire books, notably *The Prince and the Pauper* and *Personal Recollections of Joan of Arc*.

Let me repeat: the basic difficulty was that neither Mark Twain nor his readers—whether the cultivated few or the untutored public—could recognize the true source of his power. Neither of the roles that were open to him was ultimately congenial. His best writing belonged to a different universe from that of the "Phunny Phellows" with whom he was inevitably grouped in the public mind. But he had even less in common with the accepted Men of Letters—either with the first-raters like Emerson and Henry James, or the second-raters like Howells and Lowell, or the dozens of lesser talents that filled the literary magazines and the publishers' lists.

The proliferation of mass-circulation newspapers and magazines during the post–Civil War decades brought a hardening of cultural distinctions, as spokesmen for the official culture felt their authority threatened by the formation of a vast popular audience. Matthew Arnold declared that the newspapers were a principal factor in destroying the sense of reverence among the American people, especially through support of "the addiction to 'the funny man.'"[14] Thus the industrialization of newspaper publishing probably elicited as a defense the more and more emphatic demands for "reverence," and created a situation in which critics who wished to express an intuitive recognition of Mark Twain's importance as a writer could do so only by ascribing to him the characteristics of a Man of Letters. This maneuver resulted in some unacknowledged modification of the stereotype: Mark Twain could, for example, be called "the Lincoln of our literature," with the implication that, like the venerated President, he also showed how a man of the people, without formal education, could make himself acceptable by conventional standards.[15] But for the most part the well-intentioned efforts to demonstrate that Mark Twain was not a humorist in the ordinary sense of the word merely distorted his image and disguised the true value of his work.

The tensions involved are clearly observable in the proceedings at the ceremonial dinner staged by George Harvey, president of Harper and Brothers, Mark Twain's publishers, to celebrate the writer's seventieth birthday in 1905. Needless to say, the press coverage was favorable, not to say fulsome. The New York *American & Journal* (William Randolph Hearst's paper), calling Mark Twain "The World's Most Famous Humorist," had declared in an anticipatory article that

> in . . . varied ways has his life been cast, each year broadening and deepening his experience; and it was long ago that the mere humorist was merged in the philosopher. The effect of such a career on the kindly heart and keen, observant nature of the man has been to build greater things than the present generation has as yet appreciated, generous as its judgment may have been. It will remain for later critics to view his work with a surer vision, knowing nothing, perhaps, of that great part of his contemporary public who asked only that he be "funny," and write him down in his rightful place, between Dickens and Thackeray—America's greatest student of human nature and common life.[16]

The writer of this article, it will be noticed, was proposing to assimilate Mark Twain's work to the then highly esteemed mode of literary realism. "Philosopher" is taken to mean a writer with a "keen, observant nature" which gives him insight into human character. The "kindly heart" is thrown in for good measure, as a kind of period ornament. It would reappear frequently in the journalistic homage elicited by Harvey's dinner.

In a front-page story the morning after the dinner, the New York *Times* boldly denied the supposed incompatibility of humor and high literature by calling Mark Twain "the greatest of living humorists and the uncrowned king of American letters." "All—men as well as women—," asserted the *Times,* "showed by word and manner and act that they looked upon the chief guest as the master."[17]

But the implicit contradiction was not so easily resolved. The speeches prepared for the occasion betray a covert anxiety about Mark Twain's role as a humorist, which the speakers could not help regarding as a threat to high culture. Their uneasiness finds expression in repeated allusions to the vague but portentous notion

of reverence. An example is the statement of Professor Brander
Matthews of Columbia, the ranking academic among the guests:

> I have been delighted to hear the proper praise paid to Samuel L.
> Clemens, the man, and Mark Twain, the humorist. Clemens, the
> man, more than anyone else known to me, combines a childlike sim-
> plicity with a manly sincerity. With Mark Twain, the humorist, his
> humor is always good, his humor is never irreverent, never making
> for things of ill repute.[18]

The defensive tone of these well-intentioned remarks is unmistakable. Other speakers were even more unwittingly patroniz-
ing. Kate Douglas Riggs[19] retold the well-known medieval tale of
the "strolling player, juggler, dancer, tumbler, what you will . . . a
merry fellow, who danced and tumbled for pure joy of life," followed everywhere by "a trail of laughter," who offered his devotion to the Queen of Heaven by performing "his songs, his quaint
dances, his daring leaps and falls" before an image of the Virgin
until she descended from heaven to bless him. Mrs. Riggs drew
the obvious moral: "Behold, the tumbler (but in a deeper, truer
sense the eternal mirth-maker) canonized!" She concluded: "Hail,
Saint Tumbler! Mark, Monarch of Mirth-Makers, good artist, good
friend, good American, good man!" (p. 1887).

But perhaps the most elaborate verbal choreography on the
theme of Mark Twain's humor was offered by Irving Bacheller,
author of *Eben Holden* (1900) and other best-selling sentimental
novels. Bacheller developed an allegory of American history with
theological overtones:

> We see the sons of the Puritans leave their gloomy homes and join
> the many caravans that are going West. . . . we see them forget
> their kinship to the worm: we see them find gold and something bet-
> ter—happiness—for it is a fact that real American happiness was
> first discovered in the West. . . . on the lonely plain and mountain
> they discovered God in their own hearts . . . every man became his
> own preacher . . . suddenly a wave of laughter sweeps over the
> stage from the far left. A young man has come into view, and is tell-
> ing a story. The saddened spirit of the crowd finds relief and joy in
> it. . . . The crowd began to hustle Satan toward the wings. . . . Our
> comedian scattered the bread of happiness, and dark shadows grew

less in the light of his good cheer. . . . Mark Twain [is] exorciser of demons, leader in the conquest of the great upper world of fantasy, discoverer of eternal youth. [p. 1891]

The speeches at this literary dinner are remarkably lacking in specific references to the writings of the guest of honor. Clemens' friend Joel Chandler Harris, author of the Uncle Remus stories, wrote that Clemens

has set for the young men in this age of commercialism, greed, and graft, a far-reaching example of simple, old-fashioned honesty; and following the suggestions of a heart almost too big for one body, he is the friend and champion of all who are poor and oppressed and especially of those who have no voice to speak in their own behalf. Shams shrivel before him. [p.1889]

This sounds like a nominating speech at a political convention, but it is representative of much that was said that evening. Two glosses may be needed to make Harris' remarks fully intelligible. First, the allusion to old-fashioned honesty was meant to recall the time, ten years earlier, when Clemens had undertaken a much-publicized lecture tour around the world to earn money to pay in full the creditors of his bankrupt publishing company. Second, in mentioning championship of the poor, Harris probably had in mind *A Connecticut Yankee* and Mark Twain's stinging attacks on American and European imperialism in Asia and Africa.

Anyone familiar with Hamlin Hill's account of Clemens' last decade (in *Mark Twain: God's Fool*) will be struck by the stark contrast between the Clemens of private life—lonely, bitter, raging against God, man, and society—and the figure of inexhaustible charm, warmth, gaiety, and good will who figures in the ceremonial utterances of Harvey's guests. The tributes make sense only if one regards them as versions of the powerful American myth of happiness, innocence, and benevolence. Henry Van Dyke of Princeton, for example—author of *The Story of the Other Wise Man*—offered (with unconscious irony) "A Fairy Tale for Mark Twain's Birthday" which asserted that among the gifts given to the infant Samuel at birth were

A heart of love to human kind,
And human kind to love him! [p.1893]

It is in the context of this flood of sweetness and light that Mark
Twain's little speech, early in the program, should be viewed. As if
aware of the unspoken dedication of the scheduled speakers to propriety and respectability, he reacted by asserting that he had been
born without any morals and had acquired none since. Of course
only a few dull listeners could have failed to realize that Mark
Twain's profession of wickedness was ironic, presupposing general
recognition of the speaker's blameless character. But in 1905 any
hint of moral ambiguity, on a public occasion, was so disturbing
that even Mark Twain's playfulness could not be allowed to speak
for itself. In beginning the responses Brander Matthews felt obliged
to set the record straight:

> Perhaps I can take the liberty of disagreeing a moment with the
> guest of the evening and saying that when he chooses for purposes of
> his own to suggest that he is not a moralist, he is doing an injustice to
> himself, for one of the qualities which I should pick out of his work
> more strongly than another, more particularly than another, is the
> morality of it, the essentially ethical doctrine, the natural sense that
> underlies it. [p.1886]

The professor was no doubt being very stuffy, but his objection
was not so obtuse as it might seem. For on that occasion, as intermittently throughout Mark Twain's career, under cover of irony the
writer was slipping a rebellious assertion past the censorship of de-
corum. I do not know how the connection could be proved, and
certainly I do not have the psychological and anthropological
knowledge that would enable me to act with confidence in analyzing it. But Mark Twain and his predecessors among the American
humorists often seemed to act as avatars of the mythical figure
called the Trickster, a spirit of disorder, "an epitome [in C. G.
Jung's words] of all the inferior traits of character in individuals."[20]

"The Trickster myth," says Paul Radin, is to be encountered
"among the ancient Greeks, the Chinese, the Japanese and in the
Semitic world. Many of the Trickster's traits were perpetuated in
the figure of the mediaeval jester, and have survived right up to

the present day in the Punch-and-Judy plays and in the clown"
(p. ix). Karl Kerényi observes that the Trickster figure is "the time-
less root of all the picaresque creations of world literature" (p. 176).
It is pertinent to my subject that thievery was normally one of the
Trickster's pranks (p. 178).

Evidently the conflict within Mark Twain between reverence
and the exactly contrary impulse toward mockery (represented, for
example, by his joking reference on another occasion to "the most
malignant form of Presbyterianism")[21] engaged large cultural and
philosophical issues. Let me remind you how much of his humor
had dealt with such issues. The newspapermen among whom he
had learned the rudiments of his art in Nevada and California forty
years before had flaunted bohemian manners and attitudes. Mark
Twain asserted that when he delivered one of his earliest comic lectures, to raise funds for a new roof on the Presbyterian church in
Carson City in 1864, "everybody said that the roof would cave in
. . . and mash the congregation, because I was one of those sinful
newspapermen."[22]

Reporters preposterously accused one another in print of stealing firewood carried in by fellow roomers.[23] When Mark Twain
went back to Virginia City from San Francisco on a speaking tour in
1866, his former rivals on the Virginia City *Daily Union* told their
readers that to know he was in town was "to note . . . articles that
are missing . . . silver spoons, old stoves, worn-out amalgamating
pans . . . anything smaller than a 40-stamp quartz mill."[24]

One of Mark Twain's comic devices in these early years was to
pretend, before a strange audience, to be someone else, introducing "the speaker" with the words: "I don't know anything about
this man. At least I know only two things: one is, he hasn't been in
the penitentiary, and the other is [after a pause, and almost sadly],
I don't know why."[25] In his later years, Clemens often related a
supposed incident of his boyhood (almost certainly a folktale) in
which he stole a watermelon from a farmer, discovered it was
green, and conned the farmer into giving him a ripe melon in
exchange.[26]

The incongruity between Mark Twain's pose of rascality and the
growing recognition of his importance as a writer reached a climax
in the publicity attending his triumphal journey to receive an hon-

orary degree from Oxford University in 1907. In reading what
newspapers on both sides of the Atlantic said of him on this occasion, one is impressed by the extent to which his celebrity was
linked with a phenomenon that historians of the newspaper press
have described. When the huge circulations of papers in major cities attracted advertising on a previously unknown scale, a corresponding increase in copy was called for to fill the space around the
ads.[27] Helen M. Hughes points out, in her monograph *News and
the Human Interest Story,* that pressures of this kind led metropolitan papers to redefine "news" to include much material formerly embraced in such types of printed folklore as broadside bal-
lads about ghastly murders, pseudo-scientific hoaxes, etc.[28] Even
more important, reporters, in order to fill space, could also resort
to the interview, an American invention which came into use in the
mid-nineteenth century and was exploited on a large scale there-
after. This device made possible the manufacture of copy in any
desired quantity on any desired topic.[29]

The transformation of big-city newspapers into a medium of
mass entertainment is documented fully in the Ashcroft scrapbooks
of clippings from the British press. Clemens took evident pleasure
in collaborating with the reporters in attributing to himself behavior like that of the Trickster. According to the London *Daily Express,* when he landed at Tilbury Dock on the Thames, just below
London, some longshoremen recognized him on the promenade
deck of his steamer. "They cheered him as one might cheer a king,
and the man who has made millions laugh raised his hat, bared his
magnificent white head to them, and waved his hand."[30] It happened, also, that his arrival coincided with the theft of the gold cup
awarded to the winner of the famous annual horse-racing meet at
Ascot. Clemens noted that the newsboys' posters read, "Mark
Twain Arrives; Ascot Cup Stolen," and called attention to this in a
speech before the Pilgrim Society of London. The papers made
much of the coincidence.[31]

At the Oxford ceremony in the Sheldonian Theatre, when the
venerable professor of Greek, Ingraham Bywater, led Clemens "to
the foot of the throne" to present him to Chancellor Curzon for
the conferring of the degree, "the professor began, 'Samuel Langhorne Clemens,' whereupon somebody shouted, 'Can't you spare

him some of your hair, Mark?'" The report in the London *Star* continues:

> A hurricane of laughter drowned the Latin panegyric. Scarcely had it died away when another sprite, perched on a cloud in far away Olympus, sang out, "What did you do with the Ascot Cup, Mark, my boy?" . . . Somebody wanted to know if Mark had brought his jumping-frog with him, and there was a chorus of anxious inquiries about the famous white suit.[32]

The question about the jumping frog, presumably shouted by an undergraduate, identifies Mark Twain with Jim Smiley, the champion Trickster, who made a career of duping the inhabitants of Angel's Camp with his consumptive mare that always came to life just in time to win the race; his fighting bullpup Andrew Jackson, "that to look at him you'd think he warn't worth a cent"; and of course Daniel Webster, the carefully trained frog with few visible p'ints.

Clemens kept the joke about the Ascot Cup alive on his return to the United States. When a crowd of reporters greeted him on shipboard, just before he landed in New York, he said:

> "You probably heard about the theft of the Ascot cup and the crown jewels . . . in Dublin . . . I was accused all over England of being the culprit, and since I have no character left, I seldom took the trouble to deny it. I merely told them that any good detective knowing my habits would never put the crime on me, because he would have figured out instantly that if I had been on the job I would have taken the safe as well as the jewels and would have stolen the grand stand at Ascot as well as the gold cup."[33]

The New York *Times* interviewer quoted Clemens as saying:

> "Oh, yes; I have the cup on board, and I hope some of you reporters are slick enough to help me smuggle it through the Custom House. It would be too bad to give it up after getting so close to home with it.
>
> "But I didn't get the Dublin jewels. With the character they gave me over on the other side I should certainly not have left the case. I would have taken both."[34]

Another joke of Mark Twain's, which went the rounds of the London papers, concerned his announced plans for his own funeral. He said that it would take hours to pass a given point, and that tickets would be sold with advertising printed on the back.[35]

The celebration in the British press of Mark Twain as a jester must be viewed, of course, against the background of official approval for his work as a writer. After all, he had been invited to receive an honorary degree in the company of (among others) Rudyard Kipling, Sidney Lee, Sidney Colvin, and Auguste Rodin. But the newspaper editors obviously believed that what their readers wanted most to be told about was the comic byplay between the transatlantic celebrity and the reporters. On the other hand, Charles Whibley, whom T. S. Eliot would later praise highly as a critic, probably represented a considerable body of conservative British opinion when he published an article in *Blackwood's Magazine* objecting to the emphasis of the newspapers on Mark Twain as a comedian:

For the last month London has suffered from a violent attack of hilarity. Painfully she has held her poor sides. So fiercely has she rocked with noisy laughter that her public monuments have been in danger of destruction. For Mark Twain has been in her midst, and has transmitted, through the voices of obsequious journalists, his messages of mirth. And Mark Twain is a humourist, a simple truth which nobody is permitted to forget. He is a humourist who cannot open his mouth without provoking the wonder of the world, and, thanks to the industry of energetic reporters, we have not lost one single pearl of his speech.

It is not Mark's fault,—Mark they call him, to prove their familiarity,—nor the fault of the reporters, if a word spoken by the humourist has escaped us. All the world knows that the sublime heights of fun were climbed when Mark Twain referred happily to his own funeral. . . . Mark Twain designing his own funeral! Isn't it funny? Lives there a curmudgeon who will refrain from laughter when he hears of it? Still gayer was the phantasy which accused Mark Twain of stealing the Ascot Gold Cup. There's imagination for you! There's a pretty invention! Fleet Street accepted the joke as one man, and it will be surprising if the great man's luggage is not ransacked for the lost treasure by the Customs officers of his free and independent fatherland.[36]

The epithets "free" and "independent" show that Whibley had at least a normal supply of the Victorian condescension which had colored even Matthew Arnold's "Impressions of America," published twenty years earlier.[37] Yet after venting his scorn for the newspaper reporters and looking backward in time to castigate the irreverence of *A Connecticut Yankee,* Whibley concluded, surprisingly, with eloquent praise for elements in Mark Twain's work that he believed to be of enduring worth:

> Had he never cut a joke, had he refrained always from grinning at grave and beautiful things, how brilliant a fame would have been his! When you are tired of his irreverence, when you have deplored his noisy jibes, when his funeral and his theft of the cup alike pall upon your spirit, take down his *Life on the Mississippi,* and see what perfect sincerity and a fine sympathy can accomplish. Mark Twain writes of the noble river as one who knows its every change and chance. Yet he writes of it with an austere restraint and without any desire to humanise it out of its proper character. And there is humour, too, in his descriptions,—not the tortured humour of a later day, but humour sufficient to play, like light upon shade, in the grave places of his history.

Regrettably, Whibley failed to cite an example of the humor he admired, but he leaves no doubt that this is not what he valued most in Mark Twain's writing. He quoted with enthusiastic approval the passage that culminates in description of "a certain wonderful sunset" which, the narrator says, he witnessed "when steamboating was new to me," and which held him enthralled "in a speechless rapture." Whibley observed that although the apprentice pilot "heard 'the still, sad music of humanity' when he but half knew the river," "a profounder knowledge silenced the music, and persuaded him to own, with sincerity, that he gazed upon the sunset scene without rapture, but with the understanding of an intimate."[38]

Whibley's remarks about *Life on the Mississippi* are particularly valuable because he is specific: he quotes a passage and undertakes to say what he likes about it. Yet his attitude remains obscure. For example, he seems to assert that as an inexperienced apprentice, Mark Twain (whom he identifies with the narrator) was capable of hearing the Wordsworthian "still, sad music of humanity," but the critic admires the sincerity with which the writer confesses having lost this capacity when he acquired a pilot's "profounder knowledge" of the river. Yet Whibley admires the bravura passage written by the possessor of this technical knowledge, describing the "speechless rapture" he had supposedly lost the capacity to feel. And the critic intends to present this kind of rhetoric as a praiseworthy alternative to the crude jokes of Mark Twain in London in 1907.

I am dwelling on Whibley's article because his admiration for the description of the sunset in *Life on the Mississippi* represents the taste of the established literary community. In our day the passage seems a prime specimen of the kind of bogus rhetoric into which Mark Twain's immense verbal facility betrayed him all too often when he was not wearing the mask of one of his vernacular personae, such as Huck Finn. On balance, praise like Whibley's for such conventional prose was likely to do more harm to Mark Twain than the efforts of the newspaper reporters to confine him to the role of clown.

In view of the low state of both British and American criticism in Mark Twain's day, it is perhaps fortunate that most of the efforts to claim him for high culture, like the speeches at the seventieth birthday dinner, avoided all concrete references to his writing and dwelt instead on his personality. A eulogy in the London *Daily Chronicle* is representative. Calling the American guest "the most distinguished figure in the world of English letters," the *Chronicle* continued:

> Mark Twain is the national author of the United States in a sense in which we in England at the present moment have no national author. The feeling for him among his own people is like that of the Scotch for Sir Walter eighty odd years ago, or like that of our fathers for Charles Dickens. There is admiration in it, gratitude, pride, and above all, an immense and intimate tenderness of affection. . . . The "popularity" of statesmen, even of such a statesman as President Roosevelt, is a poor and flickering light by the side of this full flame of personal affection.
>
> It has gone out to Mark Twain, not only for what he has written, for the clean, irresistible extravagance of his humour and his unfailing command of the primal feelings, for his tenderness, his jollity

and his power to read the heart of boy and man and woman; not only for the tragedies and afflictions of his life so unconquerably borne; not only for his brave and fiery dashes against tyranny, humbug and corruption at home and abroad; but also because his countrymen feel him to be, beyond all other men, the incarnation of the American spirit.[39]

Augustine Birrell, Chief Secretary for Ireland, delivered an address before the Pilgrim Society in London which essentially duplicated the *Chronicle* eulogy and also, for that matter, Brander Matthews' speech at the birthday dinner in New York. Mark Twain's humor, declared Birrell, "enlivens and enlightens his morality, and his morality is all the better for his humour. That is one of the reasons why we love him." Birrell also made it clear that he preferred sentiment to humor when he named as his favorite among the writer's works *Personal Recollections of Joan of Arc*, "a book of chivalry, of nobility, and of manly sincerity, for which I take this opportunity of thanking him." The newspaper transcript of the speech here adds "(Cheers)."[40]

As these examples suggest, English newspaper comment and ceremonial oratory about Mark Twain did not differ appreciably from their American counterparts, and the professional criticism that has been surveyed by Rodney, Baetzhold, and Welland, while offering occasional insights, did not come closer than American criticism to a grasp of the true originality of his best work. The existence of the Ashcroft scrapbooks is a strong indication that Mark Twain paid attention to what was said about him in the press. But at this high point of his fame, when he had been a subject of public discussion for many years, there is no evidence that he had been able to profit as a writer from the opinions and judgments so freely offered him. All his life he had had the misfortune to be out of phase (so to speak) with the main currents of literary theory and practice in his day, which had been moving steadily toward realism and naturalism. Even the critics who had rid themselves of such vestiges of decadent Romanticism as Whibley's fondness for a Wordsworthian communion with Nature assumed that Mark Twain ought to write realistic fiction. But his concerns as an artist lay in a quite different direction: with comic fantasy and, above all, with the inexhaustible possibilities of language—a topic that was almost entirely neglected (for example, by Howells). Thus the best critical thinking was of little more use to him than the raucous popular approval of his humor or the genteel endorsement of such efforts as *Personal Recollections of Joan of Arc.*

After *Huckleberry Finn*—to go back somewhat in time—Mark Twain seemed at a loss to find a direction in which he might move as a writer. Falling back on his inexhaustible resource of literary burlesque, he had written *A Connecticut Yankee,* but as he finished it he declared it would be "my swan-song, my retirement from literature permanently."[41] He meant to cease writing for publication and devote himself to managing the immense industry he expected to create with the manufacture and marketing of the Paige typesetter. An often quoted letter to Howells, written just after *A Connecticut Yankee* was finished, voices Mark Twain's dissatisfaction with his efforts to express himself in fiction:

> Well, my book is written—let it go. But if it were only to write over again there wouldn't be so many things left out. They burn in me; & they keep multiplying & multiplying; but now they can't ever be said. And besides, they would require a library—& a pen warmed-up in hell.[42]

The inferior quality of Mark Twain's published work during the last twenty years of his life, and the melancholy bulk of the thousands of manuscript pages that he produced but did not publish, reveal that he was in some fashion blocked, confronted by obstacles to self-expression he could not overcome. Finding himself trapped in what seemed a dead end, he devoted more and more time and energy to recording private thoughts and feelings he believed to be unacceptable to any audience and, therefore, unpublishable. He told an interviewer for the London *Times* in 1899 that he planned to devote "a great part of the remainder of his life" to "a work which is only to be published 100 years after his death as a portrait gallery of contemporaries with whom he has come into personal contact." His object would be "telling the truth . . . without respect of persons or social conventions, institutions, or pruderies of any kind." I take this to be a reference to the attitudes and policies prevailing in the world of literary journals and established publishing houses. But Mark Twain also repudiated the role of humorist:

> These portraits of men and women . . . will not be written in the style of Mark Twain's books, which their author anticipates will be forgotten by the time his gallery is published. Any humour they may contain will be entirely unsought. It must be inherent in the subject if it is to appear in the portrait.[43]

In the event, Clemens' ruminations gave less space to character sketches than to such impersonal topics as the depravity of the God depicted in the Bible and restatements of the contradictory theses that man is a machine and that the human race is hopelessly damned. After the death of his wife in 1904, he formed the habit of dictating to a stenographer, sometimes almost daily, a monologue dealing with whatever topic was uppermost in his mind. For example, he wrote to Howells in 1906: "To-morrow I mean to dictate a chapter which will get my heirs & assigns burnt alive if they venture to print it this side of 2006 A.D.—which I judge they won't." A few days later, to the same correspondent, Clemens mentioned "some fearful things . . . for no eyes but yours to see until I have been dead a century—if then. But I got them out of my system, where they had been festering for years—& that was the main thing. I feel better, now."[44]

One notes that the difficulty still seems to lie with the audience, or rather with the lack of an audience willing to accept what Mark Twain wanted to write. Having abandoned the accepted genres of fiction, he was discovering that if he tried to deal seriously with social and philosophical themes, every utterance was greeted either with laughter or with protests against his trying to be serious, when his true role was to be the funniest man in the world.

The editors in the Harper office were of no use to him. Many years later Theodore Dreiser recalled that, in 1910, Frederick A. Duneka and F. G. Leigh, of the Harper staff, told him they were obliged to "employ to the utmost their arts of discreet yet firm diplomacy, in order, as they said, to 'protect Mark' from the violent and fateful public conservatism of Americans, if not the world in general, should any of the things he was writing and bringing in ever reach them."[45] Even more to the point, perhaps, is a passage in a letter from Albert B. Paine to "Dear Bill" (probably William H. Briggs of the Harper staff), written in 1926, sixteen years after Clemens' death:

> I think on general principles it is a mistake to let any one else write about Mark Twain, as long as we can prevent it. . . . As soon as this is begun (writing about him at all, I mean) the Mark Twain that we have "preserved"—the Mark Twain that we knew, the traditional Mark Twain—will begin to fade and change, and with that process the Harper Mark Twain property will depreciate.[46]

In other words, sales would drop.

With the aid of the image of Mark Twain created by the newspapers, the Harper policy was remarkably successful in maintaining a bland surface that was thoroughly at variance with Clemens' actual state of mind during his last decade. The policy was to represent him as a composite of harmless funmaker and genial lover of mankind. But the refusal to acknowledge any shadow in the golden glow of the writer's life and work was not peculiar to Paine and the Harper staff. The resolute optimism of Anglo-American culture could anesthetize the reading public to such texts as "Pudd'nhead Wilson's Calendar" with entries like the following: "Whoever has lived long enough to find out what life is, knows how deep a debt of gratitude we owe to Adam, the first great benefactor of our race. He brought death into the world" (epigraph to chapter 3). An obituary notice of Mark Twain in the London *Spectator* contained the following tranquil statement:

> It has been said that no man confidently believes in his religion who cannot afford sometimes to laugh about it. The necessary confidence appears in Mark Twain's belief that human life is an admirable thing, and that human foibles are lovable things.[47]

And we remember that Paine and Duneka brought out their expurgated version of *The Mysterious Stranger* in 1916 for the Christmas trade with illustrations by N. C. Wyeth, as if it were a children's book.[48]

Fortunately, the habit of dictation activated Clemens' memory and imagination to such an extent that he transformed the notion of a portrait gallery of persons he had known into an autobiographical work of epic proportions, taking off into fiction whenever he wished, and having for its structural principle the free association of ideas in the Lockean sense—that is, of images, recollections of the past. The two thousand typed pages that were the result of his work on this project over many years have been published only partially, in unsatisfactory selections by Albert B. Paine and Charles Neider.[49] The plan abandons the realistic or naturalistic novel, as that genre was practiced at the turn of the twentieth century.[50] It might rather be considered a flawed but magnificent anticipation of Proust. Once again, however, Mark Twain's failure to comprehend his own imaginative power deterred him from full realization of the project.

Hemingway's often quoted declaration is nevertheless true: with *Adventures of Huckleberry Finn*, Mark Twain's revelation of the possibilities inherent in the tradition of native humor marked a new departure in American literature.[51] The simplicity of this thesis is deceptive and has been only imperfectly understood. The power of the book is not primarily in its fable, its recital of a story of alienation and principled flight from civilization. Huck's lighting out for the Territory cannot bear the intellectual or symbolic weight that has been placed on it by critics. The book is important for traits that it shares with such apparently unrelated earlier masterpieces as "A True Story Repeated Word for Word as I Heard It" (1874) and "Baker's Blue-jay Yarn" (1880). Like the later novel, these sketches exhibit vernacular speech completely mastered and used to achieve an overall effect of unpretentious but absolute esthetic novelty. The effect is not primarily a matter of content. The "Blue-jay Yarn" is overwhelmingly funny; "A True Story" builds an authentic pathos despite its melodramatic plot.

The seminal impulse from *Adventures of Huckleberry Finn* is in its language. To this extent at least, we may profit from the linguistically oriented French critics. Mark Twain's use of Huck's dialect as the controlling narrative medium frees the book from the constraints imposed by the decadent system of values we call (after Santayana) the "genteel tradition." This act of destruction, whose profundity is partially concealed by the fact that it was performed in the unpretentious guise of humor, provided a new perspective

on the materials of fiction. As Neil Schmitz asserts in a highly stim-
ulating recent book (*Of Huck and Alice: Humorous Writing in
American Literature*), it created a space, a linguistic and therefore
a literary space, within which experiment and ultimately innova-
tion became possible.[52]

Louis J. Budd

A "Talent for Posturing"

The Achievement of
Mark Twain's Public Personality

Literary critics can be refreshingly trusting. Since the Romantic movement we have followed the faith in a new kind of immortality, nobler than the fundamentalist dream of a heaven that merely transfigures the home town or a favorite landscape. This new path to preserving a personal identity lies in art that wins undying fame purely through its excellence. Furthermore, with a vengeful irony, this triumph will usually defy not only the reigning esthetic standards but also the workaday mores.

Under a defensive veneer of burlesque, the Shelleyean hero of Thomas Wolfe's *Look Homeward, Angel* learned to live by just such a faith, which still carried two lesser doctrines that we seldom examine squarely. First, though a touch of late popularity during an artist's lifetime may foretell eternal glory, mass applause will usually turn out to be ephemeral. Second, worthwhile fame has to come in the "total absence of mystification and management," a bouquet James Fenimore Cooper laid on the backwoods renown of the Deerslayer; has to come on its own, without any welcome, much less connivance. As Mark Twain said in his seventieth year, to underline a skeptical argument, "I wish I could be that young again." Nevertheless, many who condescend to his mind as simplistic about mainstream or practical affairs believe that fame, if allowed to operate in the long run of classic laissez-faire economics, proves how good the artist was; therefore, to court it is not simply to act undignified and crass but to disturb the workings of esthetic justice. Guiltily, Frost devotees try to swallow the fact that he was such a dogged and shrewd PR man for his poetry.

The faith or hope that widespread fame comes without, at the minimum, the artist's cooperation has to ignore how public opinion typically works, especially after mass literacy created—or was seduced into—what Henry James deplored as the age of "newspapers and telegrams and photographs and interviewers." Most Ph.D.s in English still approve, instinctively, James's shudders at the torrent of daily print and image. They condemn it as an anti-humanistic force and are proud of refusing to read the social scientists, or even the cultural and intellectual historians, who are struggling to develop theories of mass communication. However, we do not have to agree on a rationale of the underlying process in order to develop a case for the constructive effects of the tremendous prestige that Twain came to enjoy during the last twenty-five years of his career.

Many priests in the temple of literature reject Twain just because they see him as wallowing in publicity with unholy glee. I intend to make them angrier yet, before offering what impresses me as more than adequate consolation. To put the matter bluntly, Twain did not just welcome publicity: he eagerly sought it for almost fifty years, starting with its lower form of notoriety, once he signed on with the Virginia City *Territorial Enterprise* in 1862. Courting it expertly yet candidly and succeeding beyond all precedent, he made the prestige of Irving and Longfellow look provincial or classbound. The courtship jars even some esthetic Populists because they cannot settle for a Sandburgian warmth of proclaiming that the people had followed an innate meta-wisdom or for a depth historian's analysis of conceding that Twain had stumbled upon a geyser of collective hungers. Of course, oversimplification is all too possible. His fame interacted with a network of publics—regional, socially vertical, culturally hostile to each other, sharply varied in literacy—which kept evolving but always insisted on some values that he must not violate. Luck also played its part; the vagaries of collective opinion sometimes startle even the cockiest manipulators. Nevertheless, the most productive approach is to center on Twain's campaign to promote himself into an applauded figure. Its ultimate justification is that it created a culture hero who was supportive for his own day and, though we may stand too close to judge with balance, constructive for a long time to come.

Though the notion of Twain promoting himself is familiar enough, we have registered the *ad hoc* episodes more than the underlying process. Interest in his major books has acquainted us with his anxiety about booming the sales in any imaginable way. Likewise, those who are interested in his lecture tours can dredge up lurid examples, like his circus-style "The Trouble Begins at 8" poster in 1866. In 1895, not satisfied with the grabber of a round-the-world swing, he pressed his manager to play up its uniqueness as the first such tour undertaken to pay off debts, assumed as a point of honor. His get-rich schemes are also highlighted in a way that blurs the continuity of his business activities. Whether we like it or not, he thought of his now-revered signature as a logo—a brand name, even—rather than a pen name. As early as 1873, at an attorney's suggestion, he started trying to establish "Mark Twain" as a protected trademark, like, say, Plantation Bitters, a product he admired for its gimmicks of advertising. In 1908 he finally set up, with legal nuts and bolts, the Mark Twain Company. Between those points lay a line (in several senses) of products riding on his name—a Self-Pasting Scrapbook, a Memory Builder or a History Game, calendars, and postcards with his picture, autograph, and a maxim. He openhandedly gave his permission for other commodities, though it is not clear whether he directly approved, with or without a fee, Mark Twain Cigars, Mark Twain Tobacco, Mark Twain Whiskey, or a Mark Twain Mazurka and Mark Twain Waltz. When hopes ran high, he probably wished that the ill-fated typesetter was named after him too.

We resent his moneymaking, which did keep drifting toward disruptive anxiety about his investments, and would like to forgive it as schizophrenic, queerly cut off from his best writings. Likewise, we can forgive his showboating as a boyish holdover, redeemed partly because it allowed him to create a Tom Sawyer and Hank Morgan. Such tolerance has led us to underrate the power of a tradition that he fully comprehended and exploited to support his first major step ahead of the pack of journalists who were trying, literally, to make a name for themselves. The tradition can be most recognizably based in Davy Crockett as that of the uproariously colorful character, an "original" impudently aware of shocking the earnest citizenry while his admirers cheered in the spirit of know-ingly lending a hand to the game. They allowed such characters to combine some version among the roles of showoff, folk oracle, and spokesman for popular enthusiasms and to draw a living from the transaction as a box-office performer, elective official, promoter of speculative ventures, columnist, or freelance wit. Twain, having observed the game since boyhood, plunged into it full tilt at his first chance. For the *Territorial Enterprise* of 10 January 1863, toy-ing with the editorial "we" while reporting his supposedly brash behavior at a charity ball, he bragged explicitly, "We were feeling comfortable, and we had assumed an attitude—we have a sort of talent for posturing."[1]

Because of the similarity in names, he would particularly watch the brash career of George Francis Train during the 1860s. Closer to his own talents, he perceived that the newspaper humorists worked up to the lyceum circuit whenever they could. Of course the shining example was Artemus Ward, the showman posing as showman. For solvency the lyceums depended on fresh drawing cards, like another comic journalist, Petroleum V. Nasby, and stage-wise veterans, ranging from John Gough, the often reformed drunk-ard, to Victoria Woodhull Claflin, who trailed scents of free love. Some competitors doubted the Reverend Henry Ward Beecher's genuineness well before his trial for adultery. In short, Twain's self-promotion fitted into a going pattern that includes his antics on the platform. Even the stern-faced, didactic lecturers put up with catchy advertising. His grievous sin, in their eyes, was that he egged on the hoopla, as he had been doing since he gave up on mining.

By 1863 he had already staked out, or so he boasted to his family, the "widest reputation as a local editor, of any man on the Pacific coast." Soon he had more specifically established Mark Twain as a lively figure "whose way of reporting the news . . . and whose very comings and goings were themselves news." From then on he kept infusing his journalism with an "informal chronicle of his own do-ings and thoughts."[2]

Near the brilliant end of Twain's career, a few weeks before his death, a magazine editor who had coped with him for decades dared to talk about the "evident compulsion, however genially complied with, of the openly dramatized personality." Such im-plicit criticism reflects the sedate respectability that Twain had often flouted. But this weary editor had been somewhat charmed too; for he had begun by observing, "There are no impressions of Mark Twain that are not personal. The world is full of them, as it is full of his memories, which he has generously been communicating for nearly half a century."[3]

So far, my point may sound thin to those who are posted on the scholarship about Twain. Furthermore, we all know he was a printer's apprentice in Hannibal. What we have not adequately absorbed is how long he considered himself an experienced, and still (or almost) a practicing journalist. More cogent here, we have not analyzed what his newspaper days taught him about popularity and its link with reality, as mediated by the press, or in other words about the dialectic between reputation and substance. As a pillar of Nook Farm, he took little interest in celebrities—that is, persons well known for being well known. He understood that process too well. Instead he cheered for demonstrably solid achievers: Grant the general, Stanley the explorer, Rogers the marshal of industry and finance. Most apropos here, we have not searched for the lessons, defensive and aggressive, that journalism taught him about the tricks of achieving fame, which he turned into herohood, though even his streak of grandiosity had not aimed that high. He managed so well because his inside knowledge wised him up early, spelled out the unwritten rules of the game, and taught him to ride out the inevitable bad breaks and tricky winds.

When, late in his crowded life, Twain wondered if there was anybody important whom he had not met, the world of journalism was a poor arena for challenging his smugness. Almost as much from old loyalties as self-interest, he customarily proved affable to editors and the reporters they sent out. He often proclaimed his membership in their guild during a speech to some press club. He still did so after he no longer needed to charm reporters—after they respectfully admitted they were now a nuisance in his case. Visiting Boston in 1905, he opened a two-hour interview by "reminding the newspaper men that since beginning with his pen at 14, he had never been able to regard himself as really out of journalism." Socializing at the office of the Baltimore *Sun* in 1907, he described himself as "beyond dispute the oldest journalist in the country," because "ever since the time I first began the business with my little paper in Hannibal, Mo., I have been in newspaper work, with scarcely any interval whatever, in one form or another."[4] To help clothe this tall statement, he included serving as the "subject of newspaper comment," by then so plentiful that we will never find all of it.

Though ten years of working experience could have taught Twain the ins and outs of publicity, the notion that he left journalism behind with the Buffalo *Express* by 1871 needs refining. For pay or self-satisfaction he regularly turned up in a newspaper column. In 1878 he may have weighed the advantages of going back into harness with the Hartford (Conn.) *Courant*. When Joseph Pulitzer entered the New York City market in 1884, his editor thought of Twain as the rival *Herald's* humorist. That overstated the case by far, but now and then he still tossed off a sketch for some daily journal. When his cash ran low in the early 1890s, he cranked out a series of travel letters from Europe that tried to revive the magic of *The Innocents Abroad*. Almost solvent by 1897, he nevertheless accepted a deal to cover the procession on Queen Victoria's Diamond Jubilee for the New York *Journal*, then seriously discussed a contract with its owner, William Randolph Hearst, for a weekly article. Soon after that he cabled an eyewitness story from Vienna to Putlitzer's *World* and later whipped up a feature article for its Sunday magazine. In 1902, though wealthy again, he supplied the New York *Herald* with a comic color story on the America's Cup races. It is symptomatic, or at least curious, that when the steamship carrying him home from the supreme triumph of his Oxford degree had a minor collision, he scored a beat by radioing a factual story to, apparently, both the Hearst and Pulitzer papers. In his opinion, anyway, he never lost the reporter's knack, and he probably reckoned that he could fall back on some kind of journalism if everything else failed.

Since self-hatred figures in biographies of Twain, we might expect his later attitudes toward the newspapers to ride on sarcasm. But beneath some fiery complaints he kept his respect for the standards and democratic mission of the American press.[5] Furthermore, the metropolitan dailies, especially after 1885, competed far more sharply than today, and he was devoted to their product, both the morning and evening editions and, of course, any "Extra."

His lecture manager in Australia wondered if Twain's literary taste had become "depraved through the reading of newspapers, to which he is addicted almost as much as to smoking bad cigars" (in fact, he particularly enjoyed the two together). His challenge, "I'd like to see the cigar I couldn't smoke," led the manager to the parody, "I should like to see the newspaper he could not read."[6]

A fair encapsulation of his attitudes is his verdict on W. D. Howells' "newspaper man [Bartley Hubbard], who is brought before the public a second time in 'Silas Lapham.' He is a wonderful creation, a photograph of many such men who do exist, not a cheerful, nice sort of man to sit at a communion table perhaps, but still a strong, living man."[7] Twain had a realistic sense of the skepticism, pushiness, thick skin, and opportunism that bring success to reporters. But, to narrow toward my immediate point, he also had a vigilant sense of their power to make or break a reputation in their headlong rush for copy that would strike the editor as likely to catch the reader's eye.

Sam Clemens was surprised by the impact of the humor that he unloaded on local citizens through the Hannibal *Journal*. By the time he led the pack in Nevada, he gloated over how much grief his squibs could bring to a mining stock or politician. Next, in San Francisco, he set out to discredit the chief of police, who decided Twain was doing so well that he must be hounded out of the city. Such episodes suggest that Twain was learning how easily reputations are puffed up or deflated, how solid they can look although they are paper thin, and how effectively ridicule operates because it cannot be crushed by rational argument—though the powerful can fight back if they have the right leverage. When King Leopold's press agents charged in 1906 that the British Foreign Office was paying Twain to harp on the atrocities in the Belgian Congo, he felt no stunned surprise; he understood the ploy and the hidden agenda. By 1895, if not before, he had racked up another of his firsts for American authors by subscribing to the services of a clipping bureau.

Throughout his career Twain commented explicitly on the workings of reputation, his own or that of others, though sometimes the line is neither easy nor crucial to draw. Because an actress was packing theaters across the country though she spoke only Italian, he exclaimed in 1867, "It beats me entirely. I believe the newspapers can do anything now."[8] His sketch "General Washington's Negro Body Servant" (1868) groaned at how editors, hungry for grist, can squander columns on a ridiculous claim to importance and thus confer notoriety. With *The Innocents Abroad* still to come, he may have privately wondered if he had stirred up more attention than he could sustain. By the 1880s he might feel that he had managed so well that his momentum would carry him over most reefs. Chapter 30 of *Life on the Mississippi* included "Anecdote illustrative of influence of reputation in the changing of opinion." A field hand opined that a "so-so" steamboat had loafed up the river, but when he was told it was renowned for speed, he recalled that it "jes' went by here a-*sparklin'*!" At some level of awareness, this anecdote reflected a confidence that surfaced clearly in 1888, as Twain lounged in Washington Square with Robert Louis Stevenson and they discussed the loyalty of an author's true fans.

Yet Twain knew that reporters are quick to dig at and share the awkward truths behind the facade, as he had done in Nevada and in Washington, D.C., where he started out as secretary to a theatrical senator. In a still unpublished item, he likewise professed to know that the author of the most reverential guidebook to the Holy Land often chuckled privately over his skill at shedding tears.[9]

As Twain's fame grew, an awareness of his own margin of faking, along with his hyperactive guilt about mistreating people, worried a conscience that had tolerated his swashbuckling of the 1860s. More important, he heard himself named in the warnings that professional humorists can count on only a brief vogue, and his Nevada years had sensitized him to has-beens dreaming about the bonanza they had let slip away. Carrying on a mini-genre that Twain himself had once raucously exploited, witty paragraphers for the newspapers competed in pouncing at a fat target. He fretted, as the exhilaration of his triumph with *The Innocents Abroad* cooled: "The papers have found at last the courage to pull me down off my pedestal & cast slurs at me—& that is simply a popular author's death rattle."[10] It took him several more years to learn not to see a trend in two consecutive instances of a story that he thought was jeering.

In our hindsight, he imagined too many crises, overestimating—for example—the fuss that his speech at the Whittier Dinner caused in 1877. In 1897, however, he got away with the greedy

mistake of letting the New York *Herald* organize a fund for dona-
tions to him. Ironically, the determination of the press, both newspapers and magazines, to cloak his bankruptcy in ethical grandeur
had encouraged this blunder in tactics. The encompassing fact is
that for almost fifty years Twain postured in the center spotlight
with shrewd mastery of the competition. Explaining Hurstwood's
failure in New York City, Dreiser's *Sister Carrie* points out there
were a "half-hundred . . . roads to distinction" and "each had been
diligently pursued by hundreds, so that celebrities were numerous. The sea was already full of whales" (chapter 30). Yet Twain
made himself the "king," dethroned only by death. In 1901 Gelett
Burgess closed his "Ballade of Dead Humourists" with

> O Wits, I'm calling a spade a spade;
>   Have done with your stunts ere your bubbles burst!
> Too much of Muchness, and you are flayed!—
>   "He's not so good as he was at first!"

But the "Ballade" did not name Twain among those who needed to
recognize that "Fame was ever a fickle jade."[11]

Admired personalities get many kinds of homage, and Howells
felt that the conductors at Grand Central Station, who rated Twain
in a class by himself, would have held up any train while he went to
the men's room. The unique difference in his case, however, proceeds from the eruptions of mass tribute. In 1889 a Boston audience applauded for minutes at his surprise walk-on; the women
waved handkerchiefs and the organist sounded a *fortissimo*. In the
summer of 1900 a false rumor of his homecoming gathered a push-
ing crowd on the pier in Manhattan. Dazzled by the habitual hub-
bub after his arrival, his daughter Clara would recall instances of
clapping as he entered the dining room of a hotel. When he went
to a football game in Princeton, the students greeted him with a
"Siss-boom-ah" and let off an occasional "Tiger" for him. (Today, a
cultural historian wavers between quizzicality and theorizing about
totems, the collective soul, or the lonely crowd hungering for a father.) When Twain came into the stadium at a bicentennial affair
for Yale, the presumably educated crowd of ten thousand rose to
their feet and cheered. When he spoke to the Manhattan YMCA in

March 1906, thousands snarled the traffic in the streets, and some swore at the police reserves who turned them away. Twain's only close competitor in popularity was Rough Rider Teddy (now President) Roosevelt. Both of them warily kept that fact in mind.

The headlined riot at the YMCA helped to build a new peak of Twain's prominence during April of 1906, when, incidentally, a "great wave of applause" for his presence interrupted a championship match at billiards in Madison Square Garden. We can take a quick measurement from the indexes to the New York *Times* and New York *Tribune,* though the entries for Twain are incomplete. Of course we also need to search the *Herald, Sun,* and *World*—morning and evening editions—and the Hearst pair, which showed just as keen an interest but usually got less cooperation from Twain than their competitors.

Collectively, these papers, joined by the struggling New York *Star* and New York *Press,* and sometimes the Evening *Post,* amplified by the metropolitan giants elsewhere and echoed by hundreds of small dailies and weeklies, were conducting a nonstop hunt for any twist or angle: for yarns out of his past or a scoop on his plans to build a house in Redding, Connecticut; for bulletins on his civic activity, such as raising money for a monument to Robert Fulton or his leading role in the reception of the radical Maxim Gorky; for more reminders of his masculine devotion to billiards or of his humanitarian side (he was quick to speak at a fund raiser for college scholarships or victims of the great San Francisco earthquake); for headlines about his universal appeal ("Mark Twain Was Wreathed in Girls") or his live-wire practicality (Twain as the best example, in a metaphor from bridge, of how to win "the Rubber in the Game of Life"). Before April ended, he got bronchitis, but that was news too, especially after he let still another photographer take shots of him reading or writing or just smoking in bed. Some of that bedtime also went into dictating his autobiography. From high spirits, but partly in truth he confessed: "I notice the people who pass along at my back [in a mirror] and whenever they say or do anything that can help advertise me and flatter me and raise me in my own estimation, I set these things down." [12]

He stared into that mirror with a compounding sense of strangeness and light cynicism. His face at times seemed remote, too famous and prestigious to belong to Sam Clemens of Hannibal. Contemplating it also reminded him of his skill at posturing to keep it widely admired. An extended passage in "Three Thousand Years among the Microbes," written during the summer of 1905, juggled a set of attitudes toward his "thoughtful and deeply reasoned arts" which "played my game" of being a "celebrity who is so shy and modest by nature that he shrinks from public notice."

Actually, Twain knew he had no reputation for shyness: that motif disguised, rather, his seasoned caution. Always alert to the dangers of overexposure, he had his "I narrator" confess, "I have copied the ways of kings; they do not make themselves common to the public eye." The total passage mixed defensiveness, embarrassment, sardonicism at the hypocrisy of those who insist they would dislike mass adulation, and pleasure in his lion's share of it. But underlying all else was the self-consciousness itself, which, as the passage says, would have been forced on him by the comments of friends in any case.

The peak of April 1906 was topped again in June 1907, when Twain went to England to accept an honorary degree from Oxford. By then, many newspapers could afford cartoons and the improved technique for printing a half-tone photograph. The surge of words and pictures held both less and more than met the eye. Less, because the press was increasingly driven to concoct the columns of stories that would save it from having too many pages that carried just advertising; more, because those stories responded to the hunger that urbanized and regimented readers felt for vicarious drama, marketed as the "human interest" side of the "news."

As early as 1895, Twain's career had achieved the status of a to-be-continued serial, an open-ended story both familiar and suspenseful. His gadding about, his troubles and triumphs, served as fodder for "bonding" conversation—the chitchat with which members of a contact group reassure each other of their shared tastes and assure themselves of being up to date. Some Twain watchers had simply jumped on the bandwagon or, less emotionally, had followed the crowd to see what the excitement was. A margin of ritual became obvious, and part of the crowd went through the motions of worship with no idea of what Twain was contributing to American culture.

However, the constant notice by the press meant also that beneath the trivia lay his unprecedented grip on the heart and mind of the public. Finally confident of that fact, Twain now and then pushed mass tolerance beyond its apparent limits, jeering at standard morals and religiosity. He defied imperialism near the height of its martial fever. In the affirmative vein, even while giving up on a disgraced Maxim Gorky, his support of egalitarian militancy outdid *A Connecticut Yankee in King Arthur's Court:* "I am always on the side of the revolutionists. . . . Inasmuch as we conducted our own Revolution with guns and the sword our mouths are closed against preaching gentler methods to other oppressed nations. Revolutions are achieved by blood and courage alone."[13]

Another way of enriching our perspectives is to recognize that his fame ran wider and deeper than literature, that it rode on adulation among millions who had not read through one of his books. Nevertheless, it had the magic touch of intimacy. As George Ade put it: "Mark Twain had a large following of admirers who came to regard themselves as his personal friends. . . . Most of them never saw him. All of them felt a certain relationship and were flattered by it."[14]

Without a stirring deed, such as Admiral Dewey's victory at Manila Bay or Lindbergh's solo flight across the Atlantic, fame rarely soars to the heights. Neither charm nor brashness alone can supply that much lift. In fact, the Crockett-showman figure eventually sinks toward seeming boorish; and Twain wisely turned away the deals that the great Barnum proposed throughout the 1870s. Moreover, while Twain, who seldom sought out poets or novelists, liked to hobnob with journalists, they are quick to suspect the motives for cordiality. During the 1880s and 1890s the New York Press Club fought off well-heeled outsiders who wanted to join. When the comic paragraphers *do* give the publicity hound a run, their stories carry an edge of contempt. Yet, almost misleadingly, an editorial in the Washington (D.C.) *Times* of 31 January 1901 proclaimed: "There is no pose, no artificiality about Mark Twain, and that is one reason why, in a convention-ridden world, he has not produced the effect that smaller men, masquerading in large suits of armor, often do." The explanation is that he had genuine substance at the core—a unique personality that was attractive to most, magnetic to many, or fascinatingly crude to a few.

The public, at the center of its intersecting and shifting circles, sensed that Twain shared many of its interests, convictions, tastes, prejudices, and even fads—to the despair of his elitist constituency today. But in erratic and sometimes contradictory ways the public wants to look up to its heroes, and Twain did his part by displaying an independence that could spring over into willfulness.

Distracted by his clowning, we undervalue his moods of asserting his autonomy and self-regard, even dignity. His letter to the New York *Sun* about "injudicious swearing" by a rude conductor on a streetcar was a preview of "Travelling with a Reformer" (1893), which brought more fan letters than usual because it laid out a game plan for triumphing over insolent or sloppy clerks. In November 1900 his formal complaint against an overcharging cab driver brought out so many reporters that references to it cropped up for the rest of his life. While he testified that the issue was plain honesty, he clearly felt more insulted than cheated.

Overall, Twain's posture as hero intriguingly mixed brashness, open faking, spontaneity, camaraderie, an air of merited substance, solemnity, and self-respect. It also managed a steady, adaptable growth; his kind and degree of popularity do not last simply because they were once deserved. Admiral Dewey frittered away colossal prestige, and Lindbergh's soured into a bothersome memory. Twain's kept rising for half a century because, even with his best books behind him, he used his other talents and opportunities so skillfully and more and more constructively.

Having discovered early his flair as a speaker, he was always quick to put it to use, often for a worthwhile cause, and the newspaper stories on the hundreds of his speeches contributed crucially to his popularity.[15] The personae swirling up from the quoted texts and the reporters' cordial fill-in deserve full analysis beyond the obvious, accumulating proof of his ability to regale all sizes of audiences, too variegated to cover with a few examples. Likewise, cross-examining our distaste for showiness, we should recognize the art in his unbending before a group of reporters with notebook in hand. By posing for himself in Nevada and California, he came East with a honed touch for what would delight their readership. Before he came to rate the space for an interview, his insider's experience fed the tactic of planting helpful stories, and in 1870 he could already propose a media nonevent. He wanted his publisher to announce a banquet when the sales for *The Innocents Abroad* could plausibly be trumpeted as 100,000; Twain would then compose a refusal for release to the press.

He regularly came up with other schemes, all topped in 1902 when he advertised for his obituaries, offering a drawing of himself by himself as the prize. His letters to the editor, stretching over almost forty years, had a cumulative impact, suspected often as contrived but accepted to some degree as genuinely concerned. Certain of publication, he also concocted at least twenty-five help-along letters for charities, civic projects, or ceremonies like Battle Flag Day or the four hundred and fiftieth anniversary of Johann Gutenberg's birth. He responded, never colorlessly, when editors did their then standard begging for Thanksgiving, Christmas, or New Year's greetings to the public. Invitingly, he could mark a personal letter to Hearst's European agent "Not Private."

As another of the Twain firsts for an author in the literary canon, he openly issued statements to the press—six that I find, besides aborted tries (like one intended to pep up the sales of his firm's *Life of Pope Leo XIII* by commenting on the decorations recently awarded by the Vatican: "Mark Twain was prostrated this morning. He was not willing to talk to the reporter sent to make inquiries & said only this. 'When I read the list of saints appointed yesterday by His Holiness, I—well, I was deeply disappointed'").[16] It would be dishonest to argue that Twain had humanistic motives for publishing the Pope's biography, but it is just as false to deny the sincerity behind his boldly using his prestige to campaign against Tammany Hall.

The more we study Twain's interplay with reporters, the less it seems either guided by them or disoriented by his spontaneity, which *did* erupt strongly enough to add its effect. We earn the right to believe that Twain, a born actor, consciously used props. In 1900 he let a Hearst cameraman catch him in a silk topper, getting his shoes shined at an outdoor stand while smoking a cigar and reading a newspaper. His daily washing and fluffing of his white hair could betray the obsession with purity that a recent biographer diagnoses, but Twain realized that cartoonists saw the mane of a literary lion, or a chrysanthemum of elderly cheer, or the halo of a secular saint, or the weathered flag of his independence. While he *did* enjoy cigars, he flaunted them, exaggerating the cheapness of his favorite brands. He also liked to pose with a pipe, preferably a corncob.

Those examples do not add up to total cynicism; he liked to pose holding a cat because he loved the species. But that white suit was strutted out on a blustery December day at the Capitol only after careful thought. Sensitized long ago by comic descriptions of his style on the lyceum circuit, he stayed alert to the impact of his physical presence, at times insisting on his whims but increasingly careful about which studio photographs to approve. In a new biography of Whitman, not an amateur at handling the press either, Justin Kaplan decides that "probably no other contemporary writer, with the single exception of Mark Twain, was . . . so concerned with systematic uses of his pictures and their projective meanings for himself and the public."[17] The portrait of Twain best known during the later 1880s and '90s was signed by Napoleon Sarony, the photographer favored by show-business people in Manhattan. With rare lapses, Twain faced the lens solemnly, anxious to avoid a foolish grin for posterity. Though current books prefer shots with ominous shadows, he usually looked rather stiff, or else a bit ethereal if the hair was backlighted. Whatever the pose, the fact that he welcomed cameras (even into a hotel bedroom) as early as 1895 separated him from the genteelists who bemoaned the reporter's lens as one further invasion of privacy by what we now call the mass media.

The record on Twain's popularity is often cluttered, if not jumbled. While there is much chaff in the more than three hundred interviews in newspapers or magazines, they compose the neatest exhibit of how he not only obliged but also courted and eventually dominated the press.[18] Practically on the scene at the birth of the journalistic interview, he first satirized it as gimmickry. But he soon recognized that its form could serve one kind of his content superbly, and doubtless he waited eagerly until editors deemed that it should reach below statesmen or a major oracle. In 1874, when he stirred up a continuing story about a hike from Hartford to Boston with his pastor and crony, Joseph Twichell, at least one barebones interview was published. Inching toward this fresh genre, despised by the old guard, some editors at first disguised it as a human-interest sketch or a news item enlivened by direct quotation. As for the hike, Twain was chortling publicly as late as April 1906 about the exposure it got.

His first full interview came in August 1876—prearranged and dignified because it was intended to help elect Rutherford B. Hayes to the presidency, rather than upgrade, as it did, Twain's standing. When his family steamed away to Europe in 1878, only one newspaper paid much notice, with emphasis on his oddity. At his return a year later, four reporters hovered at dockside, fumbling for the right tone to take with and about Twain, who tried to make sure they gave the best slant on his gestating travel book. During his trip along the Mississippi in 1882, he was genially receptive because he would soon have another travel book ready for a door-to-door campaign; but Midwestern journalists thought him surprisingly poised, nearly as imposing as anybody trailed by a private secretary. In 1884–85 the "Twins of Genius" tour with George Washington Cable left a network of interviews that will not be fully mapped until a scholar on wheels retraces the zigzag itinerary.

No newspaper was too small and no reporters too dullish for Twain, worried that his profits as entrepreneur were falling short of his hopes, to exert himself, often clowning broadly and transparently. In reaction, he soon intensified his groaning about the ineptitude of interviewers. They tended to repeat dull questions and mangle the answers, if only by failing to reproduce the nuances of his voice and gestures. Still, in spite of his souring experiences, other journalists would get their chance so long as he could talk, even with pain. Of course he had to refuse more and more often, partly to guard his leisure but also to avoid the danger of having nothing fresh left to say. The press corps, who swapped yarns about his obligingness in the past, took the turndowns as his earned right, rather than as defection to the ranks of the ultraproper (typified among authors by James Russell Lowell and Henry James), who resented the kind of literacy threatening to submerge the solid book and the unillustrated magazine, dense with useful but preachy essays.

Even after Twain began to feel secure against the loss of popularity, worrisome threats popped up, like the venomous litigation over the rights to dramatize *The Prince and the Pauper*. Calling in the reporters often struck him as the best way to broadcast his side.

Four other reasons could produce an interview anytime, anywhere. First, his ebullience or a mood could start his mill going; a visit to the Capitol in 1889 evoked reminiscences about his stint as a freelancer there. Second, his sympathy for reporters, paid on a cheap scale of inches printed, regularly broke down his resolve to talk only on firm ground rules and only for his own purposes. Third, his temperament responded to an unusual pitch, such as from a journalist (young Rudyard Kipling) who pleaded he had come ten thousand miles for the privilege. Fourth, his heatedness on an issue, particularly the copyright laws, was always ready to boil.

Whatever his motives, he had passed over to the commanding position. Editors wanted the interview at least as much as he did, though it might be plugging *A Connecticut Yankee* or carrying on a quarrel. After his private, invited visit with the Emperor of Austria-Hungary in 1899, his manner could seem almost as royal. Still more significant for practical results, he usually dominated as the better-experienced party. He anticipated the likely subjects, volunteered his answers to unasked questions, and soared over the pitfalls, calmer than the oldest or brassiest reporter. These effects were already clear in the interviews he granted from Cleveland, Ohio, to Madras, India, to Capetown, South Africa, during his world tour of 1895–96.

The peaks of quantity came in October 1900 and June–July 1907. He expected both instances and was masterful when he was surrounded by the open notebooks. In 1900 he carried off the playlet of an exile returning gratefully to his native soil. Actually, Twain had regular spells of feeling that life in settled Europe went more bearably than the turmoil of democracy (also, he had stayed abroad throughout most of the 1890s). But his responses to the press dispelled any taint of desertion and laid patriotic ground for his anti-imperialist crusading three months later. Having struck bathetic or tragic chords several times since his bankruptcy, he also made sure to sound downright jaunty for his years. The composite effect radiated quixotic seriousness or grave comicality in a game of reader's choice. While the tactical challenge in 1907 was simpler, a top performance demanded finesse. He had to sound duly impressed with the precedent-shattering honor of his Oxford degree and maintain the dignity of a Yankee ambassador to a castle of Old World culture; but this role had to blend with reminding the British that their pomp did not faze a democrat and assuring his countrymen that no honor could make him go high-hat. The consensus in America felt that his statement to the press, after a chat with the King and Queen at a garden party, hit the perfect note—unawed yet appreciative, self-respecting yet restrained by proof that Americans knew how to mind their manners.

Twain had long since decided that the interview was a standard means of communication to his unseen audience. If a message got garbled, he fiddled with the tuning and arranged a rebroadcast. He never gave up on the medium. Urged to lie low during a quarrel within his household, he jotted "short statements of what I would have *liked*" to comment and scrawled a five-page self-interview (not the first time he had eased his mind that way). While sold on the medium, he had plausibly begun, as early as the 1880s, to think he could do better on his behalf than the results he was seeing. The interview he composed before his daughter Clara's wedding in 1909 struck most reporters as good enough to turn in as their own work.

Nevertheless, he continued to hold forth for them, either because of whim or an unusual case, as for the correspondent for a leading Italian newspaper who was invited up to Stormfield as a house guest. Still posturing, Twain startled him with a parting thought at the railroad station: "I am the king of the buffoons; I am a dangerous person."[19] Over the years, he had already granted interviews that appeared in French, German, Hungarian, Russian, and Swedish.

By now I may have dispirited even the Twain enthusiasts, especially those whose concept of the self centers on a solitary, chaste integrity, embodied by—to use his contemporaries—the Jamesian heroes who insist on wanting nothing for themselves, though their illegitimate cousin, the cowboy vigilante-sheriff, basks in a ring of gratitude, and though their workaday disciple dreams that the greedy world will see the light and force prosperity upon him. But to get quizzical about this hot-house bulb of ideals is to seize the low ground, morally, and Twain too could rhapsodize about altruism. A stronger, positive rationale can be built for him on the interpersonal school of psychology. Currently unfashionable, that school conducts its therapy on the principle that the important "you" is not the private, often hidden self but the ragged composite of how you act toward other human beings—most simply, of how you treat them or, on a larger scale, of how you function within your social context, defined primarily as the present but extended to the consequences of your behavior for future generations. While the inward-directed climber toward ethical purity feels racked on the slopes of his Everest, the hot plains crawl with shrewd and assertive sinners, and it takes courage to hang in there too.

An interpersonal psychology can console those who shudder at Twain as the hostage of his need for approval but admire his public presence. An exterior view, confined to just the marketplace, could argue that winning the support of the masses proved healthier than servitude to the rich monthly magazines (the more we learn about Richard Watson Gilder of the *Century*, the greater our dismay at the patterns he forced on authors). Likewise, scrambling for the salary of top yes-man to a generation of tyrannical, capricious newspaper moguls—such as Charles A. Dana, the younger James Gordon Bennett, Pulitzer, and Hearst in New York City—would have allowed Twain far too little autonomy. In spite of the stern prescriptions for what Twain *should* have done and therefore *become*, perhaps he understood his situation best: charming the public brought more contentment than the genteelists would have arranged for him. Still, the most respectworthy case for the outward-oriented Twain can invoke his role within society, meaning not acceptance of the ancient permafrost but leadership toward vitalizing and renegotiating the social contract.

At his simplest, Twain brought instinctual pleasure and release to millions. High culture sniffs at such capers, and even an H. L. Mencken cannot rout its cerebral austerity. Any concession hedges with the insistence that buffo humor, always nearby in Twain's writings or performances, is brutish and that the most intellectualized comedy still ranks as inferior to tragedy, which only a Philistine or a computer would suspect of self-pity. At another massive extreme, Twain grew into an avatar of the American spirit. With only his mild encouragement, he was acclaimed after 1895 as the quintessence of native qualities, certainly itemized attractively on his model and handier for humanistic than aggressive ends.

Futilely, he *did* confront the dilemmas of patriotism, such as how to act when one's own country starts an unjust war. On the everyday level, when not playing up either to chauvinism or the instinct for wild amusement, he exemplified a pattern of friendly manners and vibrant optimism that has been labeled as "American," though his international appeal suggests that it springs as much from human nature.

For many, Twain functioned as the *beau* ideal of spontaneity, of letting go without first imagining all the consequences or calculating the impressions that others will take. From the vantage point of his admirers, in strict logic, his posturing need not cancel out his spontaneity: one can try to project any quality, and indeed Twain also liked to pretend he was a bumbling fake (even at pretending). In any case, the superintendents of propriety complained that he was undermining their sermons on deliberate thought and action. The photographs of him in bed, his flannel nightshirt wrinkled, had a slightly shocked fascination for layout editors. A portrait painter who digressed for a sketch of the same pose was surprised by the interest it aroused.

The masses were heartened by, and a few individualists tried to imitate, his swagger of unpredictability, of defiance toward orderliness. The nonverbal or perhaps id-level found reassurance in his gusto with the physicalities, the nerve-end pleasures, but also the grossness and corruptions of the body. Maybe some of the rarefied explications of *Huckleberry Finn* are trying to dress up, or else to pay the duty on, subliminal delight in Huck's tactile, pungent world.

Among still more of his contemporaries, Twain functioned as the champion for authenticity, for loyalty to one's origins, to inbred values, whatever the lures of snobbery. This idea also can pass through the needle's eye of logic without pleading that Twain genuinely shared many tastes of the masses and many esthetic, social, and political beliefs of the evolving consensus (as did most authors whose niche in the academic canon is sacred). Admittedly, he sometimes faked a popular attitude or muted a hostility (toward Theodore Roosevelt, especially) that spat into the wind. Besides belaboring himself for cowardice, he more than made up for it by applying the doctrine of irreverence to encrusted routine, devout hypocrisy (as in "The War Prayer"), injustice that passes as kindly wisdom, and authority that does not earn the obedience it demands. In 1901, while so surrounded by good will that it seemed cruel to spoil the mood, he lashed out at the pieties and legalistic fictions of imperialism. Overall, his irreverent authenticity, his call to a self-respecting vision of current events, had more democratizing impact than his echoes of equalitarian slogans. Beneath any historical abstractions, he was a stimulus toward confronting oneself quizzically, even sardonically.

Twain's manipulation of his image doubtless blurred his sense of identity and aggravated the flounderings in fantasy during his closing years. Inescapably, he boggled at the mismatches between his private behavior and the white-haloed hero featured by the newspapers and magazines. His awareness of status beyond human deserving, as well as his anxieties about managing to cling to that exposed pinnacle of success, churned up surges of contempt and resentment toward mass humankind, who can seem foolishly easy to charm—or manipulate like a machine—but pitiless in their demands for more fun and unpredictable in their zigzags of taste.

Although these tensions created benefits for us as readers, some worshippers of *Adventures of Huckleberry Finn* resent Twain's drive for popularity as a personage because the energy it used might have generated another masterpiece or two. But I welcome the tradeoff of having for certain the full-blown personality—with the speeches, interviews, newspaper and magazine stories, and other memorabilia of the Twain myth as a bonus. To make peace with the probabilities may lead us to realize, furthermore, that the writings could not have arisen out of a substantially different style of life, even one planned by a committee from a Department of English.

We can today compound our benefits from that life and the personality it left behind. For an era that is flattening us out through patterns of consumption and electronic bureaucracy, Twain holds up a model of achievable individuality—and does so in Thoreau's nick of time. Twain's era is still familiar enough for us to identify with it. Yet it has distinctly passed. Having celebrated the hundredth birthday of *The Adventures of Tom Sawyer* (during the American bicentennial), we now approach that of *Huckleberry Finn*.

Twain offers a rallying point for a shared tradition just when it is being discarded more briskly than ever. Because of the uniquely varied origins integrated into both his art and conduct, he also can help us bring closer together the world of orality, which transmits some wisdoms and pleasures from folk culture, and the world of print, which is attenuating into flickering images stored on reels that may themselves be stored a thousand miles away. To academics he offers the surest path for crossing the gap between elite and popular audiences, for abandoning the ghetto from which high culture watches the technicians of efficiency shape the future without it. Twain not only expresses, but embodies, the comic genius at all levels, from the kinetic up to subleties of wit that can stretch any mind.

James M. Cox

Life on the Mississippi

Revisited

I should first explain my title. It has been more than fifteen years since I wrote about *Life on the Mississippi*.[1] I then sought the formal connections in the book that would betray a coherence beneath the drifting and disparate current of narration. Failing to find enough of them to satisfy my craving for literary unity, I tended to conclude that the book, though remarkable in parts, could not really stand by itself. And so, in dealing with it in my book on Mark Twain, I treated "Old Times on the Mississippi" as a separate entity precisely because it offered sufficient focus and form to represent a complete moment in Mark Twain's progression toward and away from what I, along with most other critics, determined was his masterpiece: *Adventures of Huckleberry Finn*. My determination determined me to use Mark Twain's long account of his return to the river in *Life on the Mississippi* as little more than a preview of Huck Finn's adventures. This time I want to see the book as a book in the life of Mark Twain.

Given its title, it ought to be a book about life on the Mississippi River, yet anyone who has read it realizes that, though it is about the great river running out of and through the heart of the nation, it is just as much a book about the life of Mark Twain. No, that is not quite right. It is rather a book in which the life of Samuel Clemens is both converted and enlarged into the myth of Mark Twain. But there is more. We cannot read this book—or any of

Mark Twain's books—without helplessly participating in and even contributing to this myth, for all his works, rather than being ends in themselves, seem means toward the end of mythologizing their author. Thus I shall begin by suggesting how both we and he have collaborated in creating the myth.

No one would deny that we have mythologized Mark Twain as a native literary genius—and that "we" is not merely the popular audience but the academic or literary audience as well. The very fact that two audiences always come to mind in our thinking about Mark Twain indicates how profoundly Mark Twain (as the name implies) divided and still divides his audience. He was, after all, a popular writer and at the same time a great writer. He was recognized as such in his own time and remains so recognized to this day. And as such he represents a division—almost a contradiction—for there is more than a little doubt on both sides of the equation whether the two identities are not mutually exclusive. We on the academic side are even more prone to see the mutual exclusiveness, it seems to me, than those who love Mark Twain as a popular writer.

This initial or "master" division is but an index to a host of divisions Mark Twain has both represented and excited. There are the embattled arguments about whether he is Western or Eastern, vernacular or genteel in identity; whether he is a journalist or an artist, a writer or performer, a confident voice of the people or an embittered misanthrope; and finally whether he is an author or a businessman. Far from being of recent vintage, these arguments, or some of them, took shape in Mark Twain's lifetime; and in the work of Paine, Mencken, Brooks, DeVoto, and Henry Smith they were developed, intensified, and refined. Their persistence until this day reminds us of how deep the divisions have always been.

Equal to the divisions, and even controlling them, is a unity of a very special kind. The reason the persistent divisions have attracted adherents is that Mark Twain always seems to occupy both sides of each division. If there was some underground rift, there was nonetheless the single public personality operating under an exposed pen name—a personality which seemed in his own time, and seems in our time too, to be larger than his writing, or at least seemed and seems not confinable to what we are pleased to call literature. It was just this larger figure that spent itself in lecturing, investing, philosophizing, advertising, and tycooning in the expansive age of finance capitalism in which he had his being. We see, and Mark Twain's contemporary audience saw, the divisions because Mark Twain in both his lecturing and writing railed at his own involvement in such "extra-literary" activity. At the same time, there was a single Mark Twain who never even tried to conceal Samuel Clemens (though Samuel Clemens on occasion recklessly tried to conceal Mark Twain) because the pen name, even as it exposed the divisions, nonetheless contained them. The containment was managed through a humor and a clarity that perpetually disarmed the anger and the contradictory complexity the divisions somehow generated.

To face Samuel Clemens' pen name is not only to see the divisions Mark Twain's audience saw but also to see the figure of the author who projected them. Much as we might wish to see this author in the businessman's or lecturer's role of betraying his "literary" career, making the writer in him subordinate to the businessman or speculator or inventor also in him, there remains a Mark Twain who emerges before us as nothing but writing. To read his notebooks is to see him turning everything at hand into writing. If he is traveling, it is never to take a vacation to get away from his "profession" but to turn every trip and every observation into a book.

Of course it is possible to say that the books aren't literature so much as padded filler to meet the subscription contracts he had entered into, as if writing were a business instead of a profession. There is no gainsaying such an evaluation; not even Mark Twain could gainsay it as he struggled to complete the books on time (and "completion" for him often meant filling out or up a number of pages even as he angrily knew his inspiration tank was dry) for the best market moment. Yet if he could not gainsay the evaluation, he nonetheless had a deeper knowledge that something about the whole realm of what had come to be called literature in the nineteenth century was confining, even suffocating, for the figure he all but helplessly knew himself to be. The literary world was a world that, in its refinements, became filled with grown-up one-horse men, whereas the world toward which he journeyed was to be occupied by boys he would imagine in a mythic form much larger than the race of men that descended from them. Moreover, this author of boyhood knew that he would always be freer and larger than the books he wrote. In other words, the books, rather than effacing him and thereby becoming representations of his authorship, or dramatizing him and thereby reducing him to a character, were made to *enlarge* him precisely because they could not contain him.

By way of touching upon this enlargement, I want to stress just how the East–West division, though it has constituted a continual critical debate about Mark Twain's identity, is actually a very reduced image of the geographical space Mark Twain mythically occupied. Such an axis—accentuated by the criticism and contention of Brooks and DeVoto—fails to take into account the North–South axis that Mark Twain also occupied. For Mark Twain touches all four points of this country's compass. Small wonder that he would finally wish to girdle the world in *Following the Equator* even as he was beginning to imagine fantasies of polar seas.

If we look at Hannibal, Missouri, where Samuel Clemens grew up, we see that it is on the Mississippi River, which was then flowing south into slavery. At the same time, it is just far enough north to be where West was South and East was North—since the Missouri Compromise of 1820 had polarized the country on a North–South axis along the line that surveyors Mason and Dixon had driven west in the eighteenth century. That political axis came to dominate the identity of his home state and village. And if the drift of the river of his youth was directly north to south, dividing east from west (as the Appalachian Mountains, running south–southwest, had previously divided them), the stretch of river he piloted was from St. Louis due south (albeit meanderingly so) to New Orleans.

If we sketched his life out of this historical and geographical configuration, we could say that Samuel Clemens fled (or deserted or escaped) the political North–South axis, once it completely volatilized, to go West where he would find a pseudonym with its origins inescapably in the river world he had left behind him, and then came into an East (which had been North) as a Westerner, there to begin reconstructing, in the age of Reconstruction, a South of Boyhood which had never existed but which he made the most real dream in our literature. That is why the language of *Huckleberry Finn*, predicated on the profound Northern sentiment of freedom, is nonetheless Southern much more than Western in its identity—which is why, by virtue of its one fatal word, it is under threat of ban to this day.

Seeing ourselves at the edge of the ban, we might be able to understand that the Concord Public Library was trying to tell us something when it banned the book upon its appearance. How wonderful that it was the Concord Library that did it, confirming just how literary the home of Emerson, Thoreau, and Hawthorne had become by 1885. I find it extremely comforting when touring Concord to remember the fact. It would never do to assault the guides with the knowledge; it is so much better to keep it in genteel restraint, at the threshold of consciousness, as one gapes at the impressive Emerson collection in the library.

But I digress. Back to the Mark Twain who at once designates the four points on the American compass and spans the time in which those four points had been confused by politics, morality, law, and finally war. If the war was the violence which clarified the morality and politics by rewriting the law, it was also the moment when Samuel Clemens found the pseudonym by means of which he reentered the Union, to which he had been a traitor, and evaded the Confederacy from which he had deserted.

He was indeed a Western outlaw in the deepest sense of the term. Of all our major writers, only Ezra Pound is a match for him in this regard. Unlike Pound, who was completing his long revolutionary poetic life when he became a traitor, Mark Twain's treason preceded his long career in prose, and, when the Civil War ended, he needed all of the humor afforded by his pseudonymous identity to disarm the moral sense of the Northeastern society he determined to enter—a society ready to judge, and even to sentence, the historic identity of Samuel Clemens.

When, after fifteen years of humorously reconstructing himself in New England society, he returned to the Mississippi in 1882 for the express purpose of writing the travel book that was to be *Life on the Mississippi*, he was at last returning in the person of Mark Twain to the river where the very term of his pen name had its origin. By the time of his return, he had made what he rightly called his *nom de guerre*, if not a household word, at least sufficiently famous that he met a steamboat of that name on the river of his youth.

He had, as we know, already returned to the river in his writing, having written seven sketches which William Dean Howells had published in the *Atlantic* (from January to August 1875) under the

title "Old Times on the Mississippi," and when he came to the actual business of writing his travel book, he inserted those sketches
wholesale. They constitute chapters 4 to 18 of *Life on the Mississippi* and are often referred to as the "first half" of the book,
though they constitute only one-fourth of its contents. These are
inevitably the chapters critics cite as the "strong part" of the book,
whereas the remaining three-fourths are often dismissed as one
more example of Mark Twain's unfortunate hauling and filling and
padding for the subscription trade. Rarely are they incorporated
into a critical vision of the book's esthetic; they are instead used by
biographers to fill out the life of Samuel Clemens.

It is not my purpose in revisiting this book to show the mar-
velous unity that is perceptible beneath the discontinuous multi-
plicity of these chapters. When I wrote my book fifteen years ago, I
think that was my purpose, and when I could not really see the
unity, I found ways of devaluing this portion of the book. I was pro-
ceeding chronologically through the work of Mark Twain, and having devoted a chapter to "Old Times on the Mississippi," I merely
used *Life on the Mississippi* as a means of beginning a discussion of
Huckleberry Finn. Unable to reduce this travel book to the closed
form literary criticism can comfortably deal with, I tended to see
the book as material with which to reinforce a critical construct of
Mark Twain's progress toward *Huckleberry Finn.* Lest I fall into
the easy indulgence of self-criticism, I should emphasize that Mark
Twain pursued exactly the same strategy in using "Old Times on
the Mississippi" to build up the very book I am revisiting.

Even so, that earlier writing, "Old Times on the Mississippi,"
seems to have more so-called unity than the travel portion of the
completed book. Being a work of memory rather than a book
worked up from travel notes, and being devoted to the more univo-
cal subject of Mark Twain's apprenticeship as a pilot, it has a more
continuous narrative line than the discursive chapters that recount
the actual return to the river. Yet anyone who truly detaches all
seven sketches and looks at them will see that there was much discontinuity in "Old Times," particularly in the last two sketches,
in which Mark Twain, departing from the Bixby-Cub vaudeville
structure to detail the nature of the pilot's power and independence, thrusts in statistics of racing times and records to accompany a string of anecdotes and historical incidents connected with

the great days of steamboating. And anyone who looks at the critical literature on Mark Twain will see that what has been most emphasized about "Old Times" is the humorous vision of Mark Twain learning to be a pilot who could "read" the river.[2] Indeed, the famous passage that invariably is trotted out of that book (as if it might be a "trot" for all future students) is the one in which Mark Twain sees the river as a text the pilot literally has to read in order to see the snags and reefs which, while dimpling the surface and adding beauty to the current, pose the threats and potential disasters that the experienced pilot's eye recognizes on the face of the water.

Such a passage, in addition to standing out as a wonderfully easy landmark for literary readers whose stock in trade is seeing the world in the figure of a text, has the summarizing clarity that is the very trademark of Mark Twain's prose. I certainly don't want to negate it, but it shouldn't be allowed to characterize either the book or the river.

At the same time, if we see why it is such a dominating passage we can by inference begin to see why "Old Times" is equally dominating in the later structure of *Life on the Mississippi*. The passage, in projecting the river as a text, shows the relation of piloting to writing. Similarly, in the career of Mark Twain "Old Times" represented (and here I am seeing it *as* the *Atlantic* sketches, not as part of *Life on the Mississippi*) that moment when Samuel Clemens, reconstructing his life under his pen name, had, in reaching the river of his youth, reached the place in his life where the name "Mark Twain" is sounded. And of course it is sounded in those sketches—once when Bixby runs the Hat Island Crossing, to the applause of an audience of experienced pilots who, having gathered to watch, have stayed to admire the feat. The call "Mark Twain" is in this instance a crisis call, not a safe-water sign. But Bixby, calm and deadpan, guides the boat through with such ease and grace that one of the onlookers says: "It was done beautiful." The second time the term is sounded, the perennially confident and complacent cub is at the wheel. By way of administering a lesson to Pride, Bixby has arranged for the leadsman to make false calls in safe water, and has also arranged for an audience to watch the fun. Hearing "Mark Twain" in what he has hitherto been confident is a bottomless crossing, the cub loses his confidence and desperately shouts to the engine room, "Oh Ben, if you love me, *back* her! . . . back the immortal *soul* out of her," only to be met with a gale of humiliating laughter from the assembled onlookers. Thus, as Samuel Clemens reconstructs his life under his pen name, he sounds the name not once but *twice* (which takes us right back to the divisions with which we began): once as a mark of the crisis so close beneath the deadpan mastery of Bixby's art, and once as a false call arranged by the master to humiliate the cub. And always this sound rings out for an audience's admiration or ridicule.

From these two moments which define the art of the master and the humiliation of the apprentice, who themselves constitute the division contained in the unified humorous reconstruction of the past (written in the waning years of national reconstruction), we can, I think, begin to see the dimensions of the world Samuel Clemens was inventing under the signature of Mark Twain. It was a world where art was a guild of master and apprentice come into the industrial age of steam; it involved both experience and memory (the master artist and pilot, Bixby, had both to know the river and to remember it); and it was art as a performance before an audience—in other words, public art, or at least art performed in public.

The signature of the author, who had once been the humiliated cub and now humorously reconstructs the past, was actually a call—a *sound*—and thus was a *sounding* in the full meaning of the word. In its original meaning it designated shallow water that could be safe or precarious, depending on whether a steamboat was approaching shallows or leaving them. The art of piloting lay precisely in negotiating depths so slight that the dangerous bottom could all but be perceived on the surface. Moreover, the greatest demands of the art were required in going downstream. In such a situation, the pilot had force behind him in the form of the natural, powerful, treacherous, and wandering drift of a mighty current he had to cross and recross as he pursued the unmarked channel forever changing on each trip he made. The art of piloting, though it all but enslaved the pilot to the current on which he rode, paradoxically conferred upon him a privilege and power that made him independent of all social and political pressures. Majestically isolate in the pilothouse, he looked with lordly freedom upon the beauty and danger of the moving river bearing him upon its current.

The pilot and his art were, as every critic of Mark Twain sooner or later comes to realize, not only the embodiment of Mark Twain's experience on the river; they were metaphors for the figure of Mark Twain the writer.[3] The remembered independence of the pilot was thus an expression of the writer's dream of autonomy and his determination to be free of conventional form. And the pilot's necessarily skeptical eye, surveying the deceptions of current and surface, was but a promise of the very identity of the writer and his pen name. For even in discussing Mark Twain's art we cannot quite tell whether we are discussing the art of Samuel Clemens. What we know, and all we know, is that there is a difference between them, a difference exposed in the text of every title page. Yet, for the life of us, we can't quite tell what the difference is. Neither Mark Twain nor Samuel Clemens could, I think, quite tell the difference—other than that a division was being signified even as a reconstructed unity was being discovered.

We can perhaps tell this much. The past life of Samuel Clemens was being humorously invented by virtue of, and by vice under, the authority of Mark Twain. The virtue was no doubt the art; the vice was no doubt the lie. And in "Old Times" the reconstruction had reached back across the division of the Civil War (which, if it had once divided the country, now divided the history of the country between the Old Republic and the New Union) to the river where Samuel Clemens could remember his youth even as Mark Twain could at last be sounded. To see so much ought to allow us to see that the signified division between Mark Twain and Samuel Clemens comes to us as a doubt—a doubt as deep, we want to say, as that with which Nathaniel Hawthorne invested his creative enterprise. But I want to say that it was and is as shallow as the depth the sounding "Mark Twain" designates. It is not a deep doubt but is right on the surface where we always see it but never know how to read it precisely because it is so easy to see and is humorously and pleasurably and clearly and easily right in front of us.

So much for the "Old Times" of the *Atlantic* sketches; now for *Life on the Mississippi*. Here the first point to see is that it is not Mark Twain reconstructing the life of Samuel Clemens as his own life but the record of Samuel Clemens returning to the Mississippi in the person of Mark Twain whom he cannot hide. In "Old Times" the *I* of the narrative, effacing both Samuel Clemens and Mark Twain in the comic act of apprenticeship played out by Bixby and the Cub, showed Mark Twain approaching the edge of fiction. It is hardly accidental that, at the time of writing the *Atlantic* sketches, he had just finished collaborating with Charles Dudley Warner on the satiric novel *The Gilded Age* (the collaboration itself signifying Mark Twain's entry into fiction, as well as his—and Samuel Clemens'—inability to write a novel by himself/themselves). But *The Gilded Age* and "Old Times" put him at the threshold of full-length fiction. As a matter of fact, even before he completed the *Atlantic* sketches he was at work on *Tom Sawyer*—the book he was to call a hymn written in prose to give it a worldly air.

In the figure of Tom Sawyer, he had indeed reached the poetic origins of youth lying behind the past of both Mark Twain and Samuel Clemens. More important, through the figure of Tom Sawyer, Mark Twain had discovered Huck Finn, whom he would release to begin his own narrative. But Huck's voice, released in the first centennial of the Republic (and surely one of the best things invented in that first centennial), couldn't complete its own story in that first surge. Instead, Mark Twain's inspiration tank ran dry.

This early portion of *Huckleberry Finn*, Mark Twain's raft book, stands in relation to the completed novel much as "Old Times" stands in relation to *Life on the Mississippi*, his steamboat book— and I think it of no little consequence that Mark Twain was actually in the process of completing both books as he returned to the Mississippi.[4] He had already begun the latter, publicly, in "Old Times" (though of course he had given no public inkling in the sketches that this was to be the beginning of a travel book, and there is no evidence that he thought of it at the time *as* a beginning). The other he had driven to the point where the raft is run over by a steamboat (a hiatus which shows, both precisely and symbolically, the two books running into each other).[5] To begin to see such a possibility is to see that it would take a trip back to the great river itself to drive the books on their parallel courses.

When he actually came to compose *Life on the Mississippi*, Mark Twain set up a casual but nonetheless definite structure, dividing the history of the river into five stages. Here is the way he asserted his structure on the fourth page of the Author's National Edition:

Let us drop the Mississippi's physical history, and say a word about its historical history—so to speak. We can glance briefly at its slumbrous first epoch in a couple of short chapters; at its second and wider-awake epoch in a couple more; at its flushest and widest-awake epoch in a good many succeeding chapters; and then talk about its comparatively tranquil present epoch in what shall be left of the book.[6]

Using his declaration of structure as a means of finishing off the three-page first stage, the river's physical history, he proceeded to devote the slight remainder of chapter 1 and all of chapter 2 to the historical history, primarily concentrating on the river's great explorers. To the third stage, the wider-awake epoch, he devoted only one chapter, despite his promise of two, and that chapter is primarily made up of the raftsman passage from *Huck Finn*. "Old Times" is converted from the seven sketches into fourteen chapters that make up the flush-times epoch. And the actual travel book, detailing the "tranquil present epoch," comprises chapters 18 to 60. His casual declaration of structure, accentuated by repeated references to writing as speaking ("say a word about," "so to speak," and "talk about"), points up the fact that the first two stages—the physical history and the historical history—take up all of 16 pages of the total 496 in the Author's National Edition. The other three stages, which Mark Twain inversely calls epochs, convert the history of the river into the life of Mark Twain.

But that is only the beginning. The two epochs that precede the travel-book account of the tranquil present epoch, constituted (as they are) of the manuscript episode of Huck Finn and the wholesale importation of "Old Times," show that even as Mark Twain was doubly capitalizing on his past published writing he was also looting his future masterpiece. Nor is that all. If we did not know that the raftsman episode had been taken out of *Huckleberry Finn*, we would never miss it; moreover, it can be inserted wholesale into that book without disturbing the narrative sequence. Of course, arguments can be and have been made as to whether the episode should be left out or put into *Huckleberry Finn*,[7] but the fact that it can be either in or out tells us more about the nature of *Huckleberry Finn* than a host of critical elucidations about its place in or out of the narrative. And beyond that, if we did not know that the chapters constituting "Old Times" were previously published as a unit, I am not at all sure that we would or could so confidently say that these chapters are the exquisite sections of the book. Knowing so much keeps us, in a real sense, subtracting from the structure and art of the book in order to add to the figural myth of Mark Twain. The only comfort I can see in this nice problem is that if we participate in making Mark Twain somehow larger than his books, we are doing just what Mark Twain himself did.

So much for the declared structure and the enlarged Mark Twain. We are still left with the devalued travel book. By way of showing how we might look at the material of the book, I want to quote its opening paragraph. Unlike the famous river-as-text passage, previously alluded to, or the "When-I-was-a-boy" passage opening "Old Times," or the "You-don't-know-about-me" beginning of *Huckleberry Finn*, this passage has never, to my knowledge, been singled out for attention.

> The Mississippi is well worth reading about. It is not a commonplace river, but on the contrary is in all ways remarkable. Considering the Missouri its main branch, it is the longest river in the world—four thousand three hundred miles. It seems safe to say that it is also the crookedest river in the world, since in one part of its journey it uses up one thousand three hundred miles to cover the same ground that the crow could fly over in six hundred and seventy-five. It discharges three times as much water as the St. Lawrence, twenty-five times as much as the Thames. No other river has so vast a drainage basin; it draws its water-supply from twenty-eight states and territories; from Delaware on the Atlantic seaboard, and from all that country between that and Idaho on the Pacific slope—a spread of forty-five degrees of longitude. The Mississippi receives and carries to the Gulf water from fifty-four subordinate rivers that are navigable by steamboats, and from some hundreds that are navigable by flats and keels. The area of its drainage basin is as great as the combined areas of England, Wales, Scotland, Ireland, France, Spain, Portugal, Germany, Austria, Italy, and Turkey; and almost all this wide region is fertile; the Mississippi valley proper, is exceptionally so.

The resonance of the passage—with its array of facts, its grandly marshaled parallelisms, and its imposing quantitative crescendo—

obscures what seems a grand joke. For right at the center of this first paragraph, and as a culminating fact about the great river's size, Mark Twain climactically announces that the Mississippi drains Delaware. This "fact," set in the majestic current of an imposing list of seemingly scientific and geographic measurements, is difficult to see precisely because it is in such a *current* of prose. If we take the passage and juxtapose it against the celebrated passage on reading the river, I think we can see how, implicitly, we are challenged to read a text.

That joke in the center of the first paragraph is equivalent to a snag in the river big enough to tear the bottom right out of a steamboat. If we have missed the snag on our first or second or third reading, seeing it instantaneously exposes what has been mere absence of vision as humiliating stupidity, and at the same time converts the feeling of humiliation into an enormous gain of pleasure as we recognize ourselves in the act of becoming master pilots. The sudden glory of our pleasure in this new-found identity shouldn't blind us to the fact that we both have and need the ignorant and complacent cub in us.

But I want to make more of this initial joke in *Life on the Mississippi* in the return visit to the book. It shows that if the Mississippi is a mighty current, so is language. The reason we miss the joke or "stretcher" is that the effect of the parallel clauses extending the size of the Mississippi carries us right by the snag. To see this force of language working is to be at the heart of narrative deception; it is also to see the function of the snag, which is nothing less than Mark Twain's deliberate deviation from a sequence of "truths" to which we have too complacently become adjusted. Those who miss the snag won't be killed, as they might be if they were pilots on the other current. They will just be comfortable jackasses, of which the world of readers is already full. Those who "get it," while they won't be sold, had better remember that they didn't always get it, and so will have a humiliatingly complacent past they have to convert into the pleasure of looking at others miss what they have lately come to see. Then there will be those who always got it—some of whom will of course be lying, whereas others will too much lie in wait, always on the lookout for every lie and every joke. And of course there will be those who insist that it wasn't much of a joke anyway, some of whom never had, and never will have, a sense of humor, and others who will be inwardly miffed that they had to have it shown them. Finally, there will be those adamant few who contend there is no joke. After all, they could say, the passage *means* to say that the Mississippi draws its water from the twenty-eight states and territories *between* Delaware and Idaho.

Read with that determination, "from Delaware on the Atlantic seaboard" is what we might call Mark Twain's redundant stutter in preparing himself to assert the area of the river's drainage basin. Against such resistance, I can't claim with arrogant assurance that this *isn't* Mark Twain's intention; I merely want to retain a skeptical eye on the passage, keeping the possibility that it might be—just *might* be—a joke.[8] It would not be a big joke, since Delaware is after all a small state; and, considering the geographical centrality I have claimed for Mark Twain, there is a rich conclusiveness in seeing him have the Mississippi "suck in" an Eastern Seaboard state. But the more important point is to see all these enumerated responses to the passage, including this last contention, as constituting an expansive humorous consciousness in Mark Twain's audience.

Seen from such a perspective of expansion, the book becomes what it is: an accumulating of every kind of narrative—Mark Twain's past, masquerading as present narrative; his importation of what he calls the emotions of European travelers as they confront the Mississippi; the broadly humorous tall tales the pilots tell him in order not so much to deceive him as to draw him out of the incognito with which he futilely tries to conceal his identity; the bogus letter of a supposedly reformed criminal preying upon the charity of gullible do-gooders wishing to believe lies (the letter, actually written by a Harvard confidence man, dressed out in the form of sentimentally appealing illiteracy); the fake narratives of spiritualists claiming to have conversations with the dead; the self-advertising lies of salesmen hawking oleomargarine and cottonseed oil as manufactured replacements for traditional substances; the intruded yarns of gamblers conning other gamblers; the romantic guide-book legends of Indian maidens (and on and on). Yet all along the way there is penetrating information, exquisite criticism of other books on the Mississippi, pungent observations of the cul-

ture of the great valley, acute commentary on the society, literature, and art of both pre— and post–Civil War America.[9] Information and history are so interlaced with tall tales, intruded jokes,
and seemingly irrelevant "loitering and gab" that truth and exaggeration scarcely can be told apart. Finally there are the episodes
that Mark Twain recounts of his boyhood as he reaches Hannibal—
narratives which biographers have all too often taken as the trau-
matic, true experience of Mark Twain's childhood, although they
have about them the aspect of indulgent (as well as invented) guilt
fantasies.

A way of seeing it all, in a bit of nubbed down compression,
would be to remember that the pilot whom Mark Twain meets on
the *Gold Dust* is called Rob Styles (the actual name was Lem Gray,
and he was killed in a steamboat explosion while Mark Twain was
writing the book). How right a name to be waiting for Mark Twain
as he hopelessly tries to hide his own identity! For Mark Twain
does indeed *rob styles*, showing us, by implication, our outlaw
writer operating as a literary highwayman, ready to raid even his
own work to flesh out his book. How much of the King and the
Duke he has in him! No wonder he comes back to that name of his
in this part of the book, showing that it had first been used by Isa-
iah Sellers (and here what is presumably the true name is nonetheless perfect), a veritable Methuselah among riverboat pilots.

Samuel Clemens had thoughtlessly yet irreverently parodied
the old man's river notes and the lampoon had, according to Mark
Twain, silenced the old captain, leaving him to sit up nights to hate
the impudent young parodist. And so Mark Twain says that when,
on the Pacific Coast, he had set up as a writer, he *confiscated* the
ancient captain's pen name. He concludes his account by saying
that he has done his best to make the name a "sign and symbol and
warrant that whatever is found in its company may be gambled on
as being the petrified truth."[10]

Never mind that Samuel Clemens didn't first use his *nom de
guerre* on the Pacific Coast (we experts see *that* joke).[11] The point
is that, if in "Old Times" Mark Twain had shown the memory, skill,
anxiety, courage, humiliation, and the joke attending the leadsman's call, he now shows the aggression, theft, parody, and comic
guilt attending the act of *displacing* the ancient mariner of the

river. Having confiscated the old man's pen name, he makes his own life and writing identical with the *epochs* of the river's emergence from the sleep of history.

The "petrified truth," which the name Mark Twain is said to signify, is itself the broadest of jokes. The actual truth is as elusive as the shape of the river that Horace Bixby had said the pilot must know with such absolute certainty that it lives in his head. Through all the shifts of perspective in this book, through all the changes of direction, the abrupt compression of space, and wayward digressions to kill time, there is yet a single writer whose shape seems somehow in *our* head, rather than in the shifting book before us. That figure is of course the myth of Mark Twain, growing out of and beyond the book that cannot contain him. We might devalue, and have devalued, this book, but in devaluing it we are already preparing to use it as a foil for *Huckleberry Finn*, the book that was waiting to be finished even as Mark Twain brought this one to an abrupt conclusion.

And this mythic figure, always materializing above his books, whose shape is in our heads, seems in his way as real as the great river—seems, indeed, to be that river's tutelary deity. He is the figure who, more than any of our writers, knows the great truth that Swift exposed in the fourth book of *Gulliver's Travels*: that if man cannot tell the truth, neither can language. Language can only lie.

In this connection, it is well to remember those Watergate days when Richard Nixon said that he would make every effort to find out "where the truth lies." Apparently, Nixon never saw the joke in his assertion,[12] but Mark Twain would certainly have seen it since he knew that the truth lies everywhere, and nothing can really lie like it. Being our greatest liar, he knew how much he believed in and needed the beautiful and powerful and deceptive river at the center of his country. It was a muddy river—the river he knew—so that you couldn't see the bottom, which was always so near, and it ran south into slavery just as man's life runs down into the slavery of adulthood. It rolled from side to side, wallowing in its valley as it shifted landmarks and state boundaries. It could hardly be bridged, and to this day has few bridges on it between New Orleans and St. Louis. It was, and still is, a lonely river for anyone upon its current. Lonely as it is, and monotonous too, it remains a truly wild river. Even now it may burst its banks and head through the Atchafalaya Bayou, leaving New Orleans high and dry. For it is a living river, always changing, always giving the lie to anyone who counts on its stability.

If Mark Twain grows out of the lie that language can't help telling, the great river grows out of some force that language cannot name. To begin to study the current of Mark Twain's prose in this book is to begin to sense the power of that other current that his discontinuous narrative displaces more than it represents. How good it is that Mark Twain does not spend all his time—he actually spends quite little—in describing, analyzing, or celebrating the river. If his book is not a great book, as great books go, it is well worth revisiting.

Revisiting it makes me know that it is time for the present generation of critics to take up Mark Twain. With their problematics, their presences-become-absences, and their aporias, they will be able to see the river as the genius loci of Mark Twain's imagination. I very much believe that this newer criticism, dealing as it can and does with discontinuity and open-ended forms, should be able to give a better account of Mark Twain's structure and language than the generation of New Critics who relied on the closed structures of lyric, drama, and novel. In the gap—I had almost said aporia—between Samuel Clemens and Mark Twain, these critics may see, as if for the first time, the writer's two I's which yet make one in sight.

TWAIN

MYTHOLOGIZES

AMERICA

AND THE

UNIVERSE

Harold H. Kolb, Jr.

Mark Twain and the
Myth of the West

The sixth American president since World War II to be born west of Chicago, Ronald Reagan chose to take the oath of office on the side of the Capitol that faces the Allegheny Mountains, and beyond them the Ohio River Valley, the Mississippi, the Great Plains, and the Rockies—rather than on the side that looks out to the Chesapeake Bay and Europe. This break with tradition helped to call the nation's attention to the West. And the West, as we looked around, seemed not only on the far horizon, but everywhere—in cigarette advertisements, clothing catalogues, television sagas, barroom bulls. But underneath this flourishing commercial surface lies a good deal of bedrock. At the time that candidate Reagan was scoring huge majorities in the Mountain States, the Census Bureau reported that the number of inhabitants in those states had risen 37 percent in the last decade, that the nation's population center had jumped to the west side of the Mississippi River. This shift in population and in political power, coupled with a developing water crisis, a reversal of policy in the Interior Department, the concentration of oil and minerals west of the hundredth meridian, and the high-riding Sagebrush Rebellion, all promise to focus our attention on the West for some time to come. Perhaps this is as it should be, for in the West lie buried not only our gold and copper and oil and coal and uranium, but also our notions of who we are. Americans like to measure themselves in the light of the Western sun.

119

For many years, especially since Turner, those who have attempted to measure the American, and the American's long shadow
cast back toward Europe, have used the term myth, a word that is
as ambiguous and complex as the West itself. Most of us use the
term promiscuously, invoking myth as "the magic ring of truth"
one moment, dismissing it as unreality the next.[1] We speak with
reverence of the myth of Diana the Huntress, with disdain of the
myth of Buffalo Bill. This terminological dispute needs to be resolved. The West, by itself, is simply a location, a vast space stretching across twenty-seven meridians of longitude. White Americans
have conceived a number of attitudes toward this location that, collectively, make up the myth of the West.

I propose to examine these several attitudes, and then I will suggest that Samuel Clemens embraces them all, that he stands astride
a complex mythology he helped to create. Thus my topic approaches
the mythologizing of Mark Twain by looking at mythologizing by
Mark Twain. The writers who have entered our mythic Olympus
have done so precisely because they have created our myths.

I   The Myth of the West

> "I've always heard these tall tales from Texas . . . Mr.
> Benedict. Just how many acres have you got, or miles or
> whatever it is you folks reckon in?"
> "Something over two million acres. Two million and a
> half, to be exact."
> —Edna Ferber, *Giant*[2]

The myth of the West embraces four theories about the nature of
the West, three of which are comparative, conceived in relation to
the East. The first is that the West was, and to a substantial extent
still is, different—different from the East, different from Europe.
The unprecedented size of Western America was the main point
made by explorers and travelers, once they discovered that they
couldn't see the Pacific from the top of Virginia's Blue Ridge Mountains. The distance from the Appalachians to San Francisco turned
out to be 2,400 miles, which would take a European traveler from
London to Moscow, with 500 miles to spare. Montana, by no

means our largest state, if moved east, would cover all of New England, plus New York, New Jersey, Delaware, Maryland, and a large chunk of Pennsylvania. For that matter, Montana is larger than twenty-seven of the thirty European countries west of Russia. But the difference of the West, according to this theory, is not just size, but also type. The geography, with its 14,000-foot mountains and painted deserts, is fundamentally distinct. "East of the Mississippi," says Walter Prescott Webb, "civilization stood on three legs—land, water, timber; west of the Mississippi not one but two of these legs were withdrawn—water and timber."[3] In this distinct geography one finds a starkness of scene and harshness of climate: blizzards and northers in winter; hot winds, chinooks, and hailstorms in summer. One also finds distinct species of grasses, flowers, and wildlife: saguaros 30 feet high, sequoias 30 centuries old, bighorn sheep, grizzlies, buffalo, cougars—as well as distinct forms of human civilization: manifold Indian cultures and such differing white subspecies as mountain men and cowboys. And through it all we encounter the characteristic Western attitudes of independence, individualism, self-reliance, pragmatism.

No one has yet dared to declare that if a man drew three treys in Syracuse, N. Y., in many a Western city the man would be blessed with a full house. The declaration has no commercial value.
—Stephen Crane, "Galveston, Texas, in 1895"[4]

The second theory of the West explicitly contradicts the first. The East, after all, has its mountains, its waterfalls, its great rivers and lakes, its ice-locked winters and searing summers. Meriwether Lewis' description of the Great Falls of the Missouri—"one of the most beautiful objects in nature . . . sublimely grand"—sounds just like his commander-in-chief's description of the Natural Bridge of Virginia: "so beautiful an arch . . . the most sublime of nature's works."[5] The deer and the lynx and the bear still roam in the East, as well as the mountain lion, which is currently making a comeback along the spine of the Appalachians. The Eastern diamondback rattlesnake is a foot longer than his Western cousin. Buffalo once grazed the Shenandoah Valley, leaving their remains scattered in the atlases: Buffalo, West Virginia, and Buffalo, Kentucky; Buffalo Lick, North Carolina; Buffalo Valley, Tennessee; Buffalo

Creek, Virginia, "so named [by William Byrd's surveying party] from the frequent tokens we discovered of that American behemoth."[6] And, at least through the eighteenth century, the East had its rich diversity of Indian cultures, from the Five Nations of the North—Seneca, Cayuga, Onondaga, Oneida, Mohawk—to the Five Civilized Tribes of the South—Cherokee, Choctaw, Chickasaw, Creek, and Seminole.

In the movement west, settlers were impelled by the same forces—a pull from the future and a push from the past—and the same human concerns—novelty, dominion, greed—that have inspired settlement everywhere. The same motives, heroic and paltry, that led to the colonizing of Virginia also opened Kentucky, and then Ohio, and then California, and then Nevada. The expulsion of the Cherokees from Georgia in 1838 established the pattern of white *Lebensraum* that was replicated for the rest of the nineteenth century in the Great Plains and the Southwest, on the Pacific Coast, and in the Rockies. According to Ray Billington, the Western mountain man "cast off the artifacts and institutions and habits of civilization," yet the main topic of conversation around the trappers' campfires, and at the yearly rendezvous, seems to have been the price of beaver hats in Paris and London.[7] Self-reliance was preached most famously in America not by the settlers of Colorado, but by the Sage of Concord. Pragmatism was cradled in New York City; Burlington, Vermont; and Cambridge, Massachusetts.[8] "The simple truth," says Edwin Fussell, "is that the American West was neither more nor less interesting than any other place . . . [until] the Great American writers—all of whom happened to be Eastern—made it seem so."[9]

One of these writers, Walt Whitman, went West in 1879 to view the land whose distinct qualities he had been celebrating for a quarter of a century. Much of Whitman's report concerns railroads, smelting works, steam sawmills, telegraph stations, hotels, and stores in "large, bustling . . . handsome cities." Whitman notes that "you can purchase anything in St. Louis (in most of the big western cities for the matter of that) just as readily and cheaply as in the Atlantic marts," and that the women of the West "are 'intellectual' and fashionable, but dyspeptic-looking and generally doll-like; their ambition evidently is to copy their Eastern sisters." Even the scenery falls short: "I took a long look at Pike's Peak, and was a little disappointed. (I suppose I had expected something stunning.)"[10] The tone here leans toward that of Stephen Crane, who made his own trip west sixteen years later. Crane equipped himself with silver spurs and "a large Smith and Wesson revolver," but he found his characteristic irony more useful:

> Travelers tumbling over each other in their haste to trumpet the radical differences between Eastern and Western life have created a generally wrong opinion. . . . It is this fact which has kept the sweeping march of the West from being chronicled in any particularly true manner.[11]

> Out where the skies are a trifle bluer,
> Out where friendship's a little truer,
> That's where the West begins.
> —Arthur Chapman, "Out Where the West Begins"[12]

A third notion about the West attempts to reconcile the theory based on difference with the theory based on similarity. The main point, according to this third view, is that the West differs from the East not in quality but in quantity. The West is an exaggeration, a pure version, the quintessence of the American experience as a whole. (Or, in a subset of this idea, the West, still in its youth, is a throwback to yesteryear, a glimpse of how things used to be in the now grandfatherly Eastern longitudes.) Thus the East is relatively spacious, but the West is vastly spacious. The East has mountains and wilderness, but the West has higher mountains, wilder wilderness. The East may have its diamondback and its timber rattler, but the West has thirteen species of rattlesnakes, as well as iguanas, horned lizards, and gila monsters. Traits that characterize Americans in general become intensified west of the Missouri. Confidence becomes brashness, optimism becomes exuberance, casualness becomes recklessness. Eastern humor is based on subtle shifts: Rip Van Winkle waking up into a new age; Western humor is characterized by the unsubtle exaggerations of the tall tale: Bemis' buffalo climbing a tree.

In 1835 Tocqueville wrote that "the principle of the sovereignty of the people has acquired in the United States all the practical development that the imagination can conceive," by which he meant that white males over the age of twenty-one who owned property could vote.[13] But Tocqueville's imagination failed to conceive how the principle of sovereignty would be extended in the West. Just after the second volume of *Democracy in America* was published, the first wagons to Oregon pulled away from Independence, Missouri, adopting as they went a Conestoga constitution that allowed all males over sixteen to vote. Those settlers who stopped in Wyoming extended the privilege to women—a half-century before the passage of the Nineteenth Amendment.

This theory of the West's representational quality has been popular with foreign commentators. James Bryce writes that

> the West is the most American part of America; that is to say, the part where those features which distinguish America from Europe come out in the strongest relief. What Europe is to Asia, what England is to the rest of Europe, what America is to England, that the Western States are to the Atlantic States.[14]

And our novelists often rely on the West as a symbol for America. When Henry James invents a history for his heavily named Christopher Newman, who is *The American,* he relates what he calls "an intensely Western story." And when, at the other end of his career, James creates another American Adam, Adam Verver in *The Golden Bowl,* he defines his nationality and his character by birthing him in a trans-Mississippi site called American City.

Thus the West, in this view, is a synecdoche—the part standing for the whole, or at least aspects of the whole. This symbolic function may help to explain the Eastern popularity of the Western tale, which carries to a dramatic extreme those qualities identified with Americans everywhere.

> Cares of the past are behind,
> Nowhere to go but I'll find
> Just where the trail will wind,
> Drifting along with the tumbling tumbleweed.
> —Bob Nolan, "Tumbling Tumbleweed"[15]

The fourth theory of the West takes a different tack, steers around the geographical and historical arguments, and asserts that, whatever the West really was, the important thing is how people perceived it. This theory has been one of the most powerful ideas in American Studies since the 1950 publication of *Virgin Land*.[16] Like much twentieth-century thought, it is rooted in the psychology of perception articulated by William James in 1890:

> Whilst part of what we perceive comes through our senses from the object before us, another part (and it may be the larger part) always comes . . . out of our own head.[17]

History is the accumulation of human behavior; behavior is controlled by perception; perception is a transaction between the object perceived and the perceiver; and the perceiver's contribution to the transaction depends on his previous experience and present needs.

In 1620 the Puritans peered westward from Plymouth and saw "a hideous and desolate wilderness, full of wild beasts and wild men."[18] Three and a half centuries later, we enacted laws to protect endangered species and to repay Indian tribes for violated treaties. In 1835 the American West appeared to be a desert, in spite of some gardenlike qualities. Three and a half decades later, it was seen as a garden, in spite of some evidence of deserts. For many years we have raced to extinguish fires in the West. Headlines have counted the acres "destroyed" while the "smoke jumper" was the hero, a peacetime warrior against the forces of chaos. Now the Forest Service has discovered that fire can be a constructive process, that many Western grasses and trees are fire-successional, and that some fires need to be protected. The tightly sealed cone of the lodgepole pine opens and releases its seeds only when heated to a temperature between 113 and 140 degrees F.[19]

Our best tale of this West, a West created by the perceiver, is Stephen Crane's "Blue Hotel." The hotel is in Fort Romper, Nebraska, a community of railroads and businessmen and lawyers, with electric streetcars soon to be built, and four churches and a schoolhouse. Into this placid community bursts a quivering tailor from New York, gorged on dime novels and convinced that Nebraska is a dangerous, hostile place, bristling with fights and bloodshed. Fearing his death—seeking his death—he finally creates a Nebraska in which his murder is not only possible but inevitable.

Somewhere in America, someone has undoubtedly listened to our songs about the tumbling tumbleweed and then picked up and left school, or job, or wife, and made a new start, feeling that he was performing a quintessentially American act. Yet the tumbleweed is a foreign import, introduced in the 1870s from Russia.

How are we to choose among these competing ideas—all of them useful, all of them, from some point of view, verifiable? Here is where the concept of myth can help. A myth is not a lie. Northrup Frye rightly condemns "the popular sense in which it means something untrue . . . as a debasing of language." Let us use *stereotype* or *cliché* for popular notions and superficial reasons, reserving *myth* for a more powerful concept: a culture's explanation of itself, of the deepest realities of human experience.

There are disagreements about many aspects of myth, about its relation to ritual, racial memory, and dream psychology, and about the existence of universal themes such as creation, fertility, or a golden age, but most of the interesting literature concerning myth converges on its embodiment of the complexities of human life— the shifting rhythms, necessary conflicts, endless choices. Myth, like tragedy, simplifies experience without reducing its complexity: contradiction is the glue that holds myth together. Robert Graves claims that the White Goddess—maid, wife, and witch—is a central myth, a claim that is supported by Northrup Frye: "Comedies derive from the phase in which god and goddess are happy wedded lovers; tragedies from the phase in which the lover is cast off and killed while the white goddess renews her youth and waits for another round of victims." Frye believes that "Graves's story is a central one in literature, but . . . it fits inside a still bigger and better known one" that is "the framework of all literature": "the loss and regaining of identity."[20]

Myths invariably attempt to set out the gains and losses embedded in the dual or triple nature of man and universe: the god who dies and is reborn; the king who is sacrificed to save the land; the world that is composed of heaven, earth, and hell; the man who is made up of flesh and spirit, reason and emotion, fear and desire. Myths generate their power precisely from their location between these opposite poles, which explains why so many of the characters in our mythic stories come in pairs: Cain and Abel, Eteocles and Polynices, Theseus and the Minotaur, Beauty and the Beast. And even solitary protagonists represent multifarious aspects of their cultures. Odysseus is poised at a moment in Greek history when strength of mind is competing with, but has not defeated, strength of body. And his career is delicately balanced between superstition and humanism, between reverence for the gods and self-reliant skepticism. Odysseus' most difficult moment is not when he faces the Kyklopês or Kirkê or Skylla and Kharybdis, but when, clinging to a broken boat in a raging sea, he is offered assistance by the goddess Ino. Take this magic sash, she says, which will give you divine protection, and dive into the sea. Odysseus thinks it over and, as Huck Finn would, decides to stick with his boat:

> Better to do the wise thing, as I see it.
> While this poor planking holds, I stay aboard.[21]

But he keeps the sash.

A modern heroic traveler achieves his mythic status in a similar manner. Charles Lindbergh became important for American culture, as J. W. Ward points out, not just because he flew the Atlantic. Others had done that, and before 1927. Lindbergh's significance derives from his ability to hold together complexly diverging concepts.[22] On one hand, his flight symbolized "the achievement of a heroic, solitary, unaided individual." On the other hand, it symbolized "the triumph of the machine, the success of an industrially organized society." Thus Lindbergh's niche in our pantheon results from his representation of apparent opposites—a quality that characterizes all our myths, all our mythic heroes. Daniel Boone, as Cooper knew, stood for both the solitary frontiersman and the harbinger of communal progress. Thomas Jefferson, a slave-owning libertarian, was our most cosmopolitan provincial. Abraham Lincoln managed to hold in suspension what Ray Ginger calls "the balanced paradoxes" of self-improvement and concern for others.[23] John F. Kennedy seemed to symbolize the best of both democracy and aristocracy. The myth of America itself complexly intertwines culture and institutions carried from Europe with those created in the New World.

The myth of the West, then, a regional version of the myth of America, is a many-splendored thing, glimmering with possibility. It is a tangled skein of ideas, simultaneously suggesting the West's differences from Eastern life, its similarities, its exuberant representation of concepts first established in the East, and its function as a Rorschach reflector of cultural needs. Single threads of this skein abound in travel brochures, frontier museums, low-budget films, and paperback novels, but our best writers have attempted to convey the full range of these complex attitudes toward the West. And that is precisely what we find if we turn to the works of Mark Twain.

II   Mark Twain and the Myth

> All our "information" had three sides to it.
> —Mark Twain, *Roughing It*[24]

Mark Twain's credentials as a Western writer are as pure as the Comstock lode. Born in a state among territories, educated on the river, Mark Twain took a postgraduate grand tour in the Far West that lasted five and a half years and gave him a vocation as a writer, a subject matter embedded in his travel experiences, and a pyrotechnic style made up of exploding rhetorical flourishes, imploding understatements, juxtapositions sharpened at both ends, and a kaleidoscope of vernaculars. All of Mark Twain's works—whether set on the Mississippi, in King Arthur's court, or in fifteenth-century Austria—have a rich and contradictory view of life that stems from the Nevada and California years, when the writer who christened himself in 1863 attempted to describe a West that was west even to a Missourian. Between Sam Clemens' departure from St. Joseph on the Overland Stage in July 1861 and Mark Twain's arrival in New York by steamer in January 1867, he wrote hundreds of news stories, sketches, and travel letters. Three years later—his apprenticeship complete, his style honed—he sat down and poured out his full tank of Western experience into his first real book.

Roughing It contains all the strands of the Western myth. The early chapters appear to be based on a theory of difference, on a West that is a wondrous new world to the uninitiated. The enthusiasm that bursts forth from the first page, like Mexican mules springing from an Overland station, plunges the reader into a landscape of sagebrush, jackass rabbits, prairie-dog villages, coyotes, buffalo, alkali flats, summer snow, and the Pony Express. Mark

Twain emphasizes the novelty of this world repeatedly. It is "curious," "new and strange," "a land of enchantment and . . . mystery." And these terms apply to the human population as well as the natural setting. Julesberg, on the South Platte River, is "the strangest, quaintest, funniest frontier town that our untraveled eyes had ever stared at and been astonished with." This novelty is intensified by the wide-eyed innocence of the narrator, who thinks that a thoroughbrace is part of a horse's leg, that drunkenness is indigestion, and that the epitome of desirable transportation is a genuine Mexican plug:

> I was young and ignorant. . . . I never had been away from home, and that word "travel" had a seductive charm for me. . . . [p. 43] I suppose I was the proudest stripling that ever traveled to see strange lands and wonderful people. [p. 96]

Yet, from the beginning, Mark Twain works to complicate this vision, to undercut the theory of difference. The naive narrator is too naive, too credulous, too pantingly eager to discover romantic novelty. When the stagecoach rolls through Scott's Bluffs Pass, the narrator thrills to see and be able to report his first experience with "genuine and unmistakable alkali water." At first, Mark Twain reports this event in neutral and matter-of-fact language, letting the naive narrator call it a "first-class curiosity" and describe its soapy appearance. Then the author begins to twist the incident in a complex process, during which a mature narrator wrests the story away from the innocent traveler. The innocent begins to gush:

> The strange alkali water excited us as much as any wonder we had come upon yet, and I know we felt very complacent and conceited, and better satisfied with life after we had added it to our list of things which *we* had seen and some other people had not. [p. 84]

Then he compares himself to the simpletons "who climb unnecessarily the perilous peaks," and we sense the voice of the experienced narrator coming through, like a palimpsest gradually growing more distinct. The experienced narrator then steps forward and unloads a crescendoing tale about simpletons that is crammed into a single, exuberant 149-word sentence:

But once in a while one of those parties trips and comes darting down the long mountain crags in a sitting posture, making the crusted snow smoke behind him, flitting from bench to bench, and from terrace to terrace, jarring the earth where he strikes, and still glancing and flitting on again, sticking an iceberg into himself every now and then, and tearing his clothes, snatching at things to save himself, taking hold of trees and fetching them along with him, roots and all, starting little rocks now and then, then big boulders, then acres of ice and snow and patches of forest, gathering and still gathering as he goes, adding and still adding to his massed and sweeping grandeur as he nears a three-thousand-foot precipice, till at last he waves his hat magnificently and rides into eternity on the back of a raging and tossing avalanche! [p. 84]

Finally, even that tale is scrapped by an ironic, pun-filled coda:

This is all very fine, but let us not be carried away by excitement, but ask calmly, how does this person feel about it in his cooler moments next day, with six or seven thousand feet of snow and stuff on top of him? [p. 85]

This passage not only provides entertainment at the expense of the innocent narrator, it casts suspicion on his enthusiasm for alkali water, his unappeasable thirst for romance, and his naive vision of an exotic West.

The exoticism of the West is diminished in other ways. The narrative thread of *Roughing It* is continually broken by references to events that puncture the place and time of the story. Mark Twain mentions a "brief sojourn in Siam, years afterward," a coat-eating camel in Syria, a passage in his "Holy Land Note-book," an article on trains in the New York *Times*. These interruptions can be laid on to an author not quite in control of his material or point of view, but they also reveal an author not willing to be saddled with a simplistic view of the West.

Even in the most carefully worked passages, those that appear to celebrate experience foreign to an Easterner, the interest often is turned from the content to the rhetoric itself. The jackass rabbit

dropped his ears, set up his tail, and left for San Francisco at a speed which can only be described as a flash and a vanish! Long after he was out of sight we could hear him whiz. [p. 53]

Two chapters later a coyote chased by a dog demonstrates a similarly preternatural velocity:

> The cayote turns and smiles blandly upon [the dog] once more, and with a something about it which seems to say: "Well, I shall have to tear myself away from you, bub" . . . and forthwith there is a rushing sound, and the sudden splitting of a long crack through the atmosphere, and behold that dog is solitary and alone in the midst of a vast solitude! [p. 68]

Here we have an author showing off (as well as a coyote), glorying in his subject not just for its own sake but for the opportunities it presents for dramatic contrast and rhetorical fireworks. The coyote, as symbol of a mysterious new land, is celebrated in one paragraph and discarded in the next, for Mark Twain's interest turns to disgust and finally a joke:

> [The coyote] seems to subsist almost wholly on the carcases of oxen, mules and horses that have dropped out of emigrant trains and died, and upon windfalls of carrion, and occasional legacies of offal bequeathed to him by white men. . . . He will eat anything in the world that his first cousins, the desert-frequenting tribes of Indians will, and they will eat anything they can bite. It is a curious fact that these latter are the only creatures known to history who will eat nitro-glycerine and ask for more if they survive. [pp.68–69]

Mark Twain thus presents us with a narrative that crackles with exuberant novelty, but one that constantly qualifies and undermines that novelty.

As the book lengthens, the view of the youthful narrator is increasingly replaced by that of an experienced adult, formerly a printer and pilot, intermittently an unsuccessful prospector, finally a journalist and man about town. The naive narrator, who "never had been away from home" in chapter 1, has become a sophisticate who "had gone out into the world to shift for myself, at the age of thirteen," in chapter 42. He continues to look for scenes and characters that would astonish a provincial Easterner—the mining boom, vice, desperadoes—but often the point seems to be that things aren't so very different after all. The fitful enthusiasms of gold and silver fever in Nevada follow the same patterns, at the same historical moment, as stock manipulations in Charles Yerkes' Philadelphia.

The shady side of Virginia City sounds a good deal like New York's "Tenderloin"—a comparison that Mark Twain invites:

> The [Virginia City] saloons were overburdened with custom; so were the police courts, the gambling dens, the brothels and the jails—unfailing signs of high prosperity in a mining region—in any region for that matter. [p. 325]

Even passages that seem predicated on a simple confrontation between East and West reveal countercurrents, west-running brooks, when examined closely. Buck Fanshaw's funeral sparkles with Mark Twain's two greatest strengths, contrast and the vernacular, fused together to give us dialogue pairings that flash with energy:

> "Are you the duck that runs the gospel-mill next door?"
> "[I am] the spiritual adviser of the little company of believers whose sanctuary adjoins these premises." [p. 299]

For all their differences, Scotty Briggs and the minister are curiously similar, not only in their linguistic parochialism but in their intersecting experiences. The minister presides at Fanshaw's funeral in an appropriate and satisfactory manner, for "the obsequies were all that 'the boys' could desire." And Scotty Briggs, a generous roughneck whose "inborn nobility of spirit was no mean timber whereof to construct a Christian," becomes a Sunday-school teacher.

Thus *Roughing It* presents a view of the West that is simultaneously different from and similar to Eastern experience. The book also provides support for the other strands of the Western myth. A tale filled with exaggerations is an appropriate vehicle for the notion of the West as exaggeration, and Mark Twain highlights the epitomizing character of life in Nevada Territory. There is nothing novel about the difficulties of dealing with bureaucratic officials, but those difficulties are magnified when red tape is stretched 2,100 miles from Carson City to Washington. Every schoolboy is taught that not all that glitters is gold (the phrase, after all, has been a cliché since the sixteenth century), but the lesson is intensified when it is learned in a goldfield. Boom-and-bust psychology

is as old as the Garden of Eden, but the phenomenon exists in its
purest form in a community in which today's grubstaked roustabout
may be tomorrow's princely nabob. And some of the narrator's adventures prove that he is reading into, not out of, the Western landscape. Thinking they are lost in the desert, in a snowstorm at night,
the narrator and his companions sink into the oblivion of death
(and Bret Harte's prose), only to discover the next morning that
they are fifteen steps from an Overland station. Experience, the
narrator learns, even in the West, is often what you think it is—an
idea reinforced by the discovery that the condescending Eastern
traveler is in turn condescended to by Western settlers:

> All the time that he is thinking what a sad fate it is to be exiled to
> that far country, that lonely land, the citizens around him are look-
> ing down on him with a blighting compassion because he is an "emi-
> grant." [p. 139]

Thus Mark Twain winds all the threads of the myth of the West
into *Roughing It*—difference, similarity, exaggeration, and solip-
sism—and he knots them together with his concern about their validity. The continuing focus, in this collection of short and tall tales,
is on credibility. The narrator peppers his work with comments
about its truth. Virtually every story, every chapter, contains an
aside that indicates how much or how little, why or why not, an
incident is to be believed:

> Really and truly . . .

> It is literally true.

> It is doubtless correct in all essential particulars.

> This is no fancy sketch, but the truth.

> It may be true, and it may not.

> These are actual facts . . .

> I have scarcely exaggerated a detail of this curious and absurd adven-
> ture. It occurred almost exactly as I have stated it.

I simply state the fact—for it is a fact—and leave the . . . reader to crack the nut at his leisure and solve the problem after his own fashion.

I do not endorse that statement—I simply give it for what it is worth—and it is worth—well, I should say, millions, to any man who can believe it without straining himself.

Some of these comments are attempts to mediate between what Mark Twain calls "entertaining nonsense" and "useful information," between the humorist's jestbook and the reporter's notebook, but taken as a whole—there are more than seventy such comments— they illuminate the deeper probings of the book: What can be believed, especially in a new country? How can cultural differences, or similarities, be proved? What are the sources of authority? What are the claims of book learning as opposed to experience? What sort of reality is captured by exaggeration, and by various degrees of exaggeration?

Mark Twain's answers to these questions are complicated, often contradictory. Published authorities are condemned in one chapter, parodied in another, and relied upon in a third. Many issues are left unresolved. In the three chapters concerning Slade, the division agent and outlaw, the narrator revels in the contradictions presented by an affable and gentlemanly table companion who has murdered twenty-six men:

The true desperado is gifted with splendid courage, and yet he will take the most infamous advantage of his enemy; armed and free, he will stand up before a host and fight until he is shot all to pieces, and yet when he is under the gallows and helpless he will cry and plead like a child. . . . It is a conundrum worth investigating. [pp. 103–04]

When the Indians along the Carson River accurately predict a flood, the narrator wonders: "How did they get their information? I am not able to answer the question." After his stay in the Mormon capital, the narrator confesses his perplexities:

At the end of our two days' sojourn, we left Great Salt Lake City hearty and well fed and happy—physically superb but not so very much wiser, as regards the "Mormon question," than we were when we arrived, perhaps. We had a deal more "information" than we had before, of course, but we did not know what portion of it was reliable and what was not. . . . All our "information" had three sides to it. [p. 136]

As a humorist, Mark Twain is necessarily interested in many-sided questions, and he pursues oppositions relentlessly in *Roughing It*: Cooper's noble savages and the Goshoot Indians, Mormon polygamy and gentile monogamy, blustering bravado and crest-fallen cowardice, gold and mica. But his confession upon leaving Salt Lake City demonstrates his characteristic habit as a thinker as well as his technique as a humorist, and it reveals the main point about *Roughing It*. However haphazard, however jumbled, however miscellaneous some of its parts, Mark Twain's fictional journey into the West arrives finally at the destination achieved by myth— a complex, shifting, continually questioning, three-sided vision of human experience itself.

Stanley Brodwin

Mark Twain and the
Myth of the Daring Jest

When William Dean Howells called Mark Twain the "Lincoln of our Literature,"[1] he not only paid homage to an old friend but encapsulated, in one memorable phrase, the essence of a mythologizing process which began during Twain's lifetime and is still vital today. And yet, in the face of this myth of an "authentic American . . . speaking his own dialect . . . local and western, yet continental," as V. L. Parrington states it,[2] we do not rest easy in granting Mark Twain his full literary genius. We are disturbed by his artistic unevenness; and his self-evident psychological and literary "doubleness" apparently creates more critical problems than it solves. Finally, the many unfinished works of his last years can be interpreted either as a breakdown of his always shaky narrative control or the result of confused emotional and philosophic tensions which caused him to push his literary formulas into incomplete but, like his mysterious strangers, always compelling, fantasy forms.

These brief generalizations remind us that, unlike any other American writer of equal stature, Mark Twain's work will continue to provoke controversy, especially as his work begs comparison with accepted classics like Cervantes, Voltaire, and Swift. Here the Lincolnian myth of Mark Twain takes on a universal dimension, demanding a radical critical reassessment that will explain how an American folk artist translated his native forms into a national epic

136

comedy which, like Cervantes', also created original epistemological, moral, and theological levels of meaning.

It is fascinating to note that at least one nineteenth-century critic saw the problem but could not deal with it. In an anonymous review of *Pudd'nhead Wilson* (1894), one critic wrote that other great "national humorists, like Aristophanes, Cervantes, Molière or Swift," expressed their humor in an "exquisite literary form," tempering whatever "extravagance" or "imaginative" difficulties were present. *Pudd'nhead Wilson*, though, is merely a "Missouri tale of changelings," powerful and "thrilling," certainly, but cannot be called "in any sense *literature*." He laughs "unrestrainedly" at it but throws the irksome question back to the reader: "What *is* this? Is it literature? Is Mr. Clemens a writer at all?"[3]

Unlike Matthew Arnold, the reviewer had the soul to laugh, but the consequence of this pathetic inadequacy to understand Twain's art, or to place it in a meaningful comparative context, led most critics and readers to fall back on two familiar descriptions endlessly juggled: Mark Twain was either an old-fashioned jester, Sir Dinadan dressed up as a moralist, or a moralist disguised as a jester to con his readers. It was, in fact, a literary and public con game, and Twain knew how to play it perfectly. The "Notice" to *Huckleberry Finn* (1884) says it all: "Persons attempting to find a motive in this narrative will be prosecuted; persons attempting to find a moral in it will be banished; persons attempting to find a plot in it will be shot."[4]

But, as we know, the game also caused Twain much personal anguish, despite the support he received from Howells and his fellow humorists. He *was* primarily a "serious" moralist and only secondarily a frontier humorist, albeit the most profoundly imaginative one of all, surpassing Artemus Ward and Josh Billings by virtue of his deeper insights into the foibles of human nature.[5] This achievement notwithstanding, H. L. Mencken pinned down the majority view: "With only his books to recommend him [Twain] would probably have passed into obscurity in middle age; it was in the character of a public entertainer that he wooed and won the country. The official criticism of the land denied him any solid literary virtue to the day of his death."[6] The reason of course was that Twain's "entertainer" images—saddleback rider on a frog, Wild

Humorist of the Pacific Slopes, steamboat pilot—created various mythic contours he could only compulsively reinforce. "I am a border-ruffian from the State of Missouri. I am a Connecticut Yankee by adoption," he boasted in his comic sermon-speech, "Plymouth Rock and the Pilgrims," in 1881. "In me, you have Missouri morals, Connecticut culture; this, gentlemen, is the combination that makes the perfect man" (28:88).

Although it gained him public fame, that seriocomic portrait also hindered, until the twentieth century, the development of critical principles that could effectively deal with his work as literature. Except by insisting on his obvious moral intentions, no one could show (though Howells began to lay the groundwork) how his tall-tale journalism was transformed into an original national art. Yet all these Missouri-Connecticut images form a single, self-created myth whose inner force derives from a core or "primal" fable located at its very heart.

I call this construct or primal fable the "myth of the daring jest," and its epitome is to be found in a trenchant fantasy called "The Late Reverend Sam Jones's Reception into Heaven" (1897), which Olivia, Mark Twain notes, forbade him to publish.[7] It is a kind of seemingly unimportant (though characteristic) tale that becomes, in a startlingly naked way, an abstract of a purpose writ large into the acknowledged great works. As such, it reveals metaphorically Twain's own meaning of his life's work and his self-created image as they were defined by his special role as national humorist. The fantasy has Mark Twain and a "stranger," the Archbishop of Canterbury, riding on a train which drops passengers off at either New Jerusalem or Sheol (Hell). At the New Jerusalem stop, a small preacher in Southwestern costume joins them, screeching Hosannahs as he elbows his way past the Pearly Gates. But Twain, despairing, as he prepares to travel on, with "humble and sincere gratitude" takes the Archbishop's flauntingly exposed ticket to Heaven, and substitutes his own. St. Peter, after checking the Archbishop's ticket, coldly rejects him: "Return to the train sir. Professional humorists are not allowed here." Recognizing the *nom de plume* but, ironically, not knowing the *face*, St. Peter falls back in horror at the idea of allowing such a man through the gates, and the poor Archbishop is stunned. Mark Twain, however, stands by, observing the scene with calm satisfaction:

"My *nom de plume!* Pardon me; Archbishop of Canterbury is a title, not a *nom de plume.*" This with a frozen bow.

It was all that St. Peter could do to keep his hands off of him.

"This is too much! That a person of your frivolous nature and profane instincts should conceive and carry out the daring jest of venturing across these sacred bounds was enough—quite enough; that you should add the affront of masquerading as an illustrious prelate whom all heaven is patiently waiting for and expecting to arrive today — is — water! — give me water, before I choke!"

These words did not merely astonish the Archbishop, they stupefied him. He stood a moment or two like one in a dream, his eyes wandering vacantly about and resting nowhere; until at last they fell by chance upon the brimstone-tinted pass in his hand; then he murmured in a piteous voice, and as one distraught —

"Mark Twain? — Mark Twain? Alas, there has been some mistake." [p. 113]

And so the Archbishop goes to Sheol while Mark Twain settles in with the wildly preaching Sam Jones, whose frontier language causes the exodus of the likes of Pope Alexander VI and Torquemada. Twain's "daring jest" has gotten him into Heaven where he tries to lead a "modest and inoffensive life," but to no avail. "Now in sober truth I never had said anything half as bad as some ministers had been allowed to say and no fault found. But there was just the difference—I was a layman you see, and not privileged to blaspheme; coarse speeches were permissible in some mouths, but not in all" (p. 116). In the end, Jones's preaching empties out Heaven—even the "Papal Borgias were revolted"—and all head for Hell, leaving only the Texan with Mark Twain.

On a superficial level, the tale certainly demonstrates Twain's aphorism, "Heaven for climate, hell for society," but its symbolic implications take us into the center of his most significant self-created image. It at once dramatizes the fantastic irony of the moralist who is damned to Hell by the hypocritical values of his Age, who *also* wishes to enter the "sacred bounds" denied him because of his vernacular comedy. That this Heaven, as Captain Stormfield discovers, is a burlesque of humanity's real needs, does not rob it of its true democratic function: to welcome the "bar-keepers" into the "sacred bounds" by the likes of Moses and Esau, a delightful, contradictory pair.

Still, the Jones piece contains a profound moral and theological irony which ramifies itself into countless "daring jests" that had literarily informed all of Mark Twain's secular and philosophical concerns. But it also poses a challenge to develop a critical point of view appropriate to the theological meaning in it. To do this, we must approach the problem in terms of three questions which emerge implicitly from the core of this fable. What is the "true" gospel of this profane preacher, who must lie his way into Heaven in order to be saved? What is the source or nature of these "daring jests" and the way they inform his comedy? What esthetic or critical perspective can we take to appreciate both the myth and its comic effects?

I think the best way to begin is to see that Mark Twain's attacks on Christianity and the Bible, his long and complex preoccupation with the Adamic myth and other biblical characters and ideas,[8] are but part of a large counterstructure of values he evolved in order to deal artistically with a culture he both rejected and yet was intrinsically part of. It is therefore most significant that he formed a lifelong but ambivalent image of himself as a Presbyterian minister, an occupation he seriously considered, except for the fact, as he told Orion in 1865, that his true "call" was to "literature, of a low order, i.e., humorous."[9] The task was to find a way of merging the seemingly incompatible "callings" of the ministry, no matter how corrupted by the Talmages and Beechers he so viciously attacked, with his gift for exciting the "*laughter* of God's children," as he put it to his brother. The very concept was a daring practical joke from the start, and Twain began to play it as early as 1867, when he had himself introduced to Captain Duncan of the *Quaker City* as the Reverend Mark Twain "who is a clergyman of some distinction," but who nearly spoiled the farce by slipping into "villainous slang expressions,"[10] a Sam Jones in the making.

But as the mock clergyman's skepticism about all things religious and biblical grew to massive iconoclastic proportions, his residual Presbyterian heritage, which he felt saddled with, found its own sermonic and artistic patterns in "*Narratives of generous deeds that stir the pulses*," and not from the "drowsy pulpit!"[11] A new theology was required for the artist-preacher which would speak to his audience, saturated with "blamed wildcat religions," a veritable riot of conflicting orthodoxies flourishing in a culture of growing technological secularism and combating the assaults of Darwinism on its religious faith. Thus in the 1870s and '80s, when he was formulating his personal compound of deism, determinism, and Darwin, Mark Twain also created a comic drama that was rooted in his view of man's cruel and unjust banishment from Eden, and whose consequences could be dramatized in terms of three related themes: Providence, lies, and moral reform. These persistent themes form the basis of his countertheology and became the texts and subtexts of nearly all his major work, dominating their structural forms and determining the modes of humor through which they were mediated.

Of Providence, "general" and "special," we know Mark Twain's views explicitly. He was "nauseated"[12] by the concept, as he learned it from his Sunday schools and as he observed its so-called "workings" in life. The way he attacked the idea and used it satirically throughout his work testifies to his rejection of its central theological purpose: to affirm and demonstrate that the world is controlled by a moral and rational governance. This concept, whose significance in Western religious thought can hardly be overestimated, came into Christianity through a complex Hellenistic fusion of classical theories (Heraclitus' *Logos*, Anaxagoras' *Kosmos*, and Platonic philosophy) with both Hebrew and Christian revelations of God's will shaping His harmonious creation. "All things work together for good," St. Paul declared (Rom. 8:28), and to deny this, according to one early Church Father, Clement, was to merit punishment rather than mere refutation. For Providence was above all a theodicy, a way of solving that most intractable of theological problems, the question of evil and its source.

The orthodox answer, that God permits evil only to turn it into ultimate good, received its most powerful validation from St. Augustine, in *The City of God*, and in Aquinas, who also demonstrated how the will of God acts normally through natural causes, accessible to reason, while God's direct intervention defines a miracle, accepted by scriptural authority or faith only. Both Augustine and Aquinas regarded foreordination and reprobation as special forms of providence, though insisting that God's predetermined teleology and theodicy did not thwart man's free will. These dogmas, renewed in Mark Twain's lifetime by the First Vatican

Council in 1869–70, had undergone profound changes in the Reformation, the most important being that Providence was no longer viewed primarily as a grand rational explanation for God's creation, but God's personal and benign care of humanity's practical, everyday experiences.

A fatherly, indeed paternalistic, quality now informed the determinism of Luther and Calvin: God tenderly watching over all. But by the seventeenth century the concept of Providence was absorbed into Protestant natural theology, so that its effects could be known equally by faith and/or reason. The universe was guided by God's general providence,and natural laws, while humanity was subject to His "special" providences. The power of the idea was used by both Catholic and Protestant churches in the battle against all kinds of philosophical skepticism that explained creation as ruled by blind chance or amoral determinism.[13]

This, then, was the theological ethos that Mark Twain inherited from his culture, an ethos that could not but infiltrate the consciousness of any person who was sensitive to questions of divine order and justice. The very intensity of his reaction against it is proof of how deeply it engaged his sensibility and explains, in part, his artistic and philosophic participation in the nineteenth-century controversies that arose from the conflict of the idea with Darwinism, the Higher Criticism, and other modern "heresies." Most theologians would have been horrified, but not necessarily surprised, for example, by Twain's iconoclastic religious attitudes or the theories in *What Is Man?* (1906), regarding the latter as yet another damnable secular substitute for God's moral teleology— which, in fact, it is. They would have known that by rejecting the deterministic theodicy of Providence, Twain, like any other skeptic committed to materialism but emotionally longing for spiritual values, would either be burdened with finding an adequate nontheological explanation for problems like evil and cosmic justice, or be faced with the psychological horror of accepting an essentially meaningless universe.

Yet it was not so much the abstract theology of Providence that disturbed him; rather, it was that moral, paternalistic, *caring* aspect of God's ways, which Protestant culture emphasized, that he could not tolerate, and that he was already lampooning in blunt squibs like the "Story of the Bad Little Boy" (1865), where the satiric thrust is twofold. It is among the first of many assaults against mawkish Sunday-school literature, but in showing the rise to fame and fortune of a "bad" boy, it announces contemptuous rejection of any providential system of rewards and punishment, a rejection whose psychological and theological consequences he would grapple with until the end of his life. The "daring jest" was to take this despised concept and make it the foundation of his artistic counter-theology. In this way it could function as a dynamic force, creating adventures and moral struggles for his boy heroes or giving Hank Morgan, Roxanna, and Joan of Arc the opportunities by which they could attempt to radically alter individual and historical destinies. And through the device of his human and divine mysterious strangers, situations could be created which victims from St. Petersburg to Eseldorf would regard, ironically, as beneficent forms of Providence, which nevertheless culminate in moral failure or an "appalling" cosmic pessimism.

The conspicuous exception is the genteel *The Prince and the Pauper* (1881), in which Twain conforms his historical and "twin" themes to the imperative of a happy and edifying Providence. Naturally, it remained his family's favorite, as well as a consistently popular children's book, although its graceful artistic and theological orthodoxy now appears as an isolated glow of affirmation, an understandable gesture of homage to the sophisticated culture of Hartford which helped nourish it. But it is in *Adventures of Huckleberry Finn* (1884), predictably, that we receive Mark Twain's most complete artistic exploration of the idea as we observe its controlling force on the actions of Huck and the morally complex adventures he encounters along the river. The dark superstitions and folklore that Huck, Tom, and Jim rely upon, with different degrees of success, offer a counterpointing pagan embodiment of the Christian concept, thereby expanding the novel's theological structure into a comprehensive commentary on the relationship between human freedom and the external forces which act upon it.

But the myth or concept of Providence was not simply a structural principle that Mark Twain could manipulate for his own artistic purposes, however complex. Its most significant function, in the context of his work as a whole, was to give his "daring jests" a theological framework into which two of his major preoccupations fitted organically: his belief that all human beings are born liars and that humanity is incapable of lasting reform. The theme of lies, in particular, is treated in so many forms—essays, stories, novels, speeches—that it may be said almost to constitute an independent, comic theology by itself. Here Mark Twain takes his vernacular Western tradition of tall tales and "whoppers" and transmogrifies it into a moral definition of man's original sinful nature, with both comic and tragic effects in his art.

Lies permeate every aspect of human nature and civilization.[14] They flourish in the guides and guidebooks of the Old World, in Sunday schools, in the romantic illusions about the West, in all the business and political practices of the Gilded Age, and finally in his "true" *Autobiography*, in which, Twain ruefully admitted to Howells, he soon began to lie.[15] In short, lying is so ubiquitous that the jester is compelled to advise his readers, in "Decay of the Art of Lying," that through neglect of its finer points we may be in danger of prostituting this "noble" art (19:360–68). "I ain't never seen anybody but lied," says the master liar, Huck, excepting only the Widow or Aunt Polly or "maybe Mary" (13:1), and that fairly states the matter. Only St. Joan and Luther, transcending human frailty, could never fall or lie.[16] No wonder Mark Twain imagined them in Eden, defying the temptations of Satan, whose serpent's trail, he wrote in *Innocents Abroad* (1869), is "over us all" (2:257).

We can now begin to see the main outline of Twain's integrated countertheology. Providence is the theological lie about the moral purposes of the biblical God; man, trusting to this providence, is the fallen carrier of the "trunk-lies,"[17] which assert that all noble values (freedom, heroism, even personal identity) exist when in fact they do not. Clearly, Twain's insistence on selfishness as humanity's driving psychological motivation establishes the necessity to lie in order to satisfy whatever needs that selfishness craves: self-approval, power, survival itself.

Nevertheless, Mark Twain did not treat lies solely as a manifestation of man's fallen or reprobate nature. Characteristically, he viewed lies in a double fashion. Just as the "two Providences" were offered to Huck by Miss Watson and the Widow Douglas, the path to Hell or to Heaven, two kinds of lies were rampant. In the brilliant comic piece, "Traveling with a Reformer," the resourceful Major responds to the narrator's query, "But is it ever right or noble to tell a lie?" in this way:

Yes, sometimes. Lies told to injure a person, and lies told to profit yourself are not justifiable, but lies told to help another person, and lies told in the public interest—oh, well, that is quite another matter. Anybody knows that." [22:81]

Mark Twain develops this distinction many times in his work, but never to such comic advantage as in *Huckleberry Finn,* where the two kinds of lies—and providences—fairly shape the structure of the novel.[18] As used by Huck, lies represent a form of innocent deception, the paradox of moral hypocrisy, in which his conscience becomes entangled and from which he must gain his freedom; as used by the adult world, they represent genuine hypocrisy. By counterpointing these two kinds of lies, Twain creates a dynamic tension and balance between a pre- and postlapsarian vision of life in the narrative. This tension also gives the book its most famous irony, for when Huck, the supreme liar, learns he "cannot pray a lie" and so must "*go* to hell" (13:297), he unwittingly fulfills the Widow's way of providential salvation, "ornery" as he thinks he is. But Huck is quite conscious of the consolatory nature of his lies, too, for when Mary Jane objects to his pretense of sending her love to the King and the Duke, he replies:

"Well, then, it shan't be." It was well enough to tell *her* so—no harm in it. It was only a little thing to do, and no trouble; and it's the little things that smooths people's roads the most, down here below; it would make Mary Jane comfortable, and it wouldn't cost nothing. [13:264]

The world "down here below"—a lovely vernacular euphemism for a fallen world—ironically gains its peace of mind through the moral use of lies. Huck cannot, to be sure, prevent some of the tragedies that he encounters and which make him "ashamed" of the human race, but he gives that race the only consolation and freedom it can realistically have.

But Mark Twain did not cease to offer this daring form of comic "grace" with *Huckleberry Finn.* The idea was so close to him that he returned to it almost two decades later, in 1902, when his pessimism was most intense, in "Was It Heaven; or Hell?" In this brilliantly ironic inversion of a typical Frank Stockton short story, the good doctor, pointedly called "the only Christian," preaches his morally satanic text of "Reform—and learn to tell lies!" (24:77) to the pious aunts. They "blessedly" do so, bringing consolation to their dying sister and her daughter, although a conventionally religious reader would be hard put to know whether the "Angel of the Lord," who appears at the end, will send them to Heaven or Hell. The "daring jest" becomes Mark Twain's theological challenge: What price salvation? The device of dramatic suspense is used only to make the reader confront himself and a new countertheology, and to reevaluate his received theological norms.

There remained, however, the power of the one kind of lie that would prove the most difficult of all to expose and change. This was the "silent colossal National Lie," which he described in the satirical "My First Lie, and How I Got Out of It" (1898): the lie "that is the support of all the tyrannies and shams . . . that afflict the peoples—that is the one to throw bricks and sermons at. But let us be judicious and let somebody else begin" (23:169). This lie had always existed, of course, but by the 1890s Mark Twain mounted a last assault against it as it strengthened imperialism, belief in moral "progress," the principle of the moral sense, and a benevolent deity. The essays, stories, and philosophical tracts of this period vary widely in their methods of attack against these principles, which seemed to Twain so self-evidently false; yet all had the common purpose of liberating humanity from their grip. The only trouble was that the jester came gradually to realize that his efforts were doomed. The third part of his countertheology, reform, was decisive.

In a century devoted to the idea of reform in every level of its moral and religious life, Mark Twain bore the cross of denying its fulfillment, even as he exploited its burden artistically. I count at least five strategies he developed to cope with the problem, all of which give an extraordinary comic and moral dimension to his countertheology. One could escape, kill, rationalize, or transcend the impulse to reform others, or accept its oppressiveness expediently. So Huck, with "Providence slapping him in the face" (13:297), escapes by thinking "no more about reforming" after his ordeal over Jim. The lie-filled narrator of "The Facts Concerning the Recent Carnival of Crime in Connecticut" (1876) kills his dwarfish conscience and starts in the "world anew," a murderous Adam satanically inverting the "born again" ecstasy of the revivalist religion with which Twain was so familiar. Tom Sawyer, quaking in fear during a thunderstorm, considers reform, then waits before relapsing, "for there might not be any more storms" (7:188). Joan of Arc, a divine truth-teller, is simply beyond the need for reform, although she is destroyed by the "Twelve Lies" of the society she changes. It is for her to play out the Gethsemane of Twain's countertheology. Pudd'nhead Wilson knows that "nothing so needs reforming as other people's habits," but no one in Dawson's Landing understands his cynical and often theologically pointed aphorisms. Indeed, at the heart of *Pudd'nhead Wilson* is Twain's most despairing vision relating to the fall of man and his ultimate inability to reform. This countertheological vision, developed in the racial context of the novel, turns on the daring providential "joke" of Roxy's switching the racially different babies in their cribs—with its rigid and unalterable consequences—and implies that all of American society is trapped in its unreformable lies. This is Twain's pessimistic determinism in its most classic form. And finally we have, in "The Man That Corrupted Hadleyburg" (1899), a superb artistic structure in which the satanic gambler's "providence" exposes the town's lie, forcing it to reform, but only so it will not be caught "napping" again. Its inversion of the Lord's Prayer, "Lead Us Into Temptation" (23:69), is a "daring jest" whose countertheology the town's expedient sense of morality can accept and, therefore, enter "the sacred bounds."

There was one more "daring jest" to create, and that was to place an unfallen, reform-free Satan in the pulpit. The various texts of the *Mysterious Stranger* complex ramify into several "truths": contradiction is the essence of reality; life is an "insane" dream dreamed by a useless "vagrant Thought," the "Self" (p. 405); the universe is "empty and soundless"—meaningless; and finally, in Pauline terms, the greatest liberation of all would be for man to escape the horror of his fleshly or "mud" image.[19] In these worlds the idea of spiritual reform has no meaning at all, and providence, if it exists, is a grotesque theodicy whose ironic results only corrode humanity's pitiful illusions of divine consolation.

Given this bleak landscape, the hagiography of the *Personal Recollections of Joan of Arc* (1896) glares out not only as a deeply felt need to capture the banner of literary respectability (forever eluding him) but also as a last attempt to assert the possibilities of spiritual heroism by apotheosizing a childlike yet militant saint.[20] For surely the meaning of Joan's life for Twain was in her role as a providential force of divine innocence (symbolized by the Fairy Tree), capable of reforming a society that wallows in political and spiritual malaise. The facts of her ultimate martyrdom were of course supplied to Twain by history itself, and in dealing with this subject he did not have to construct yet another fable to demonstrate human failure. But by presenting the tragedy through the recollection of the aged Sieur Louis De Conte, Twain was able to impose his personal vision on this history.

As in the *Mysterious Stranger* complex, Twain created thematic tensions between a charismatic figure bearing the "truth" and those who come to believe in that truth. Like Philip Traum or "44," Joan has the "seeing eye," capable of penetrating to the truth of human nature and historical destiny (17:180), but unlike them, she is vulnerable to the forces of lies and human intransigence, all of which lead to a providentially designed tragic end. Louis comes to recognize the "meanness of our poor human race" (18:109), epitomized in the end by the base motives of the French King, who only helps to rehabilitate Joan's character in order to validate his claim on the crown. Thus the separation between truth and lies, spirit and flesh, is just as absolute as in the Satan stories, without even a satanic laugh commenting on this dark knowledge. In the end, Louis' impassioned eulogy on Joan's divine genius does not so much record her defeat of the satanic forces that sent her to the stake, but her God-given destiny to *transcend* them. Transcendence alone could defeat the cruel theology that defined man and history. The significance of the novel is that it registers, in a completed artistic form, this concept. Twain therefore believed it to be his best (and favorite) book, even as he was exploring his cosmic themes of dreams and determinism.

By the end of the 1890s he had played his role of the artist and countertheologian to the fullest. On the one hand, his countertheology produced "daring jests" that showed how deeply his society was a fallen one; on the other, how only saints and unfallen Satans could transcend it. From this perspective, it appears that Mark Twain's daring theology formed an abyss between itself and his public images far more radical than hitherto imagined. For as his countertheology evolved, he became an artist whose work, Howells knew, required a philosophical understanding normally applied to Cervantes or Swift.

One such philosopher who could have provided it—indeed, who wanted to write his own version of *Don Quixote*—was Søren Kierkegaard. Describing himself as a "Janus *bifrons*," laughing with one face, weeping with the other,[21] Kierkegaard's existential theology placed humor in a central position along life's stages. It was nothing less than the first "stage of existential inwardness before faith," the state of mind through which man passes from an "ethical" to a purely "religious" stage of life. In his full ethical awareness, the humorist is able to deal comically with guilt, despair, doubt, and the need (through repentance) to transcend his sins. Profoundly aware of the contradictions in life, he cannot develop a living belief in, or enduring relationship to, a providential God—a painfully accurate description of Mark Twain's case. For the humorist, Kierkegaard wrote:

> constantly . . . sets the God-idea into conjunction with other things and evokes the contradiction—but he does not maintain a relationship to God in terms of religious passion *stricte sic dictus*, he transforms himself instead into a jesting and yet profound exchange-center for all these transactions, but he does not himself stand related to God. The religious man does the same, he sets the God-idea into juxtaposition with everything and sees the contradiction, but in his inmost consciousness he is related to God.[22]

This passage bears directly upon Twain's self-created image of the daring jester, and also helps us answer the questions I raised concerning the source and nature of the jests. Mark Twain had in fact become a jesting "exchange-center" for his society, but was ultimately unable to reconcile his "God-idea" with the contradictions, through a "leap of faith," of man related to God. Instead, Twain leapt into the dark, into the insoluble contradictions, while passionately trying to explain them through his countertheology. In Kierkegaardian terms, Twain was an "ethical-religious" humorist without faith. Moreover, Kierkegaard fully analyzed the two modes of humor the jester employs. One is the humor of "positive" content, injected into the ethical struggle and success in bridging the gap between the moral ideal and practice; the other is the "negative" content, which announces that the gap is unbridgeable. The tension and dialectic between these modes pervade Twain's comic vision and reflect the spiritual crises arising from the humorist's countertheology.[23] And because Twain was so influenced by the Adamic myth, I shall call these modes, metaphorically, "Adamic" and "satanic" humor. The former enables the daring jester to transcend or be protected from the contradictions, while the latter is the humor that surrenders to them, accepting the reality that God and man are "insane" as he confronts their works in history.

If Nietzsche said that God died out of pity for man, the satanic preacher in Mark Twain believed that the biblical God ought to be dead because he had no sense of humor, that "great regulator." In 1902 he made this note: "We grant God the possession of all of the qualities of mind except the one that keeps the others healthy; that watches over their dignity; that focuses their vision true—humor."[24] But we all know Satan's diatribe about man not having the "sense and courage" to use that gift which God lacked. It was always left to Mark Twain to use "that one really effective weapon—laughter"[25]—in both of its flexible modes.

This task is made explicit in *Innocents Abroad*, his first major work, through the mask of the self-styled "innocent" narrator, who is alternately exalted and disillusioned by the realities of the Old World. It is in the climactic scene, when Mark Twain's fellow pilgrims reach Lake Galilee, on which Jesus sailed and walked. Their inflamed piety collapses, however, on learning the boatman's fare. They begin to bargain but their boat sails away, and it is all Twain can do to control his gloating pleasure while listening to the pilgrims berate one another. Yet he does not wish to be "ill-natured" with them. He jibes at their hypocrisy but turns his anger back on himself, a quick exchange of emotion that neutralizes the comic contradiction: "They knew me. They knew my liberal way—that I like to give and take—when it is for me to give and other people to take." All he wishes to do is to "stir them up and make them healthy" (2:226). The humor and its "positive" content—to make men healthy—protect the wise "innocent" from the perception of the lie, which should have evoked cold contempt. Instead, the possibilities of moral change are affirmed in the face of the lie, a stance the narrator must continue to take through the purely formal struc-

tures of either frontier burlesque or satire. Indeed, the nature of
Mark Twain's revisions of the *Alta California* letters, into the finished book, indicate this.[26]

What the narrators of the early travel books and *Tom Sawyer*
do consciously, Huck does unconsciously. Perhaps the greatest
"exchange-center" in comic literature, he turns tragedy into comedy and reconciles all social and religious contradictions even as he
stands in an ironic relationship to God's providences and the fools
who worship Him. The Adamic mode triumphs in various ways,
and gives the book its steady comic vision. A familiar but striking
example is the sermon Huck hears during the feud (guns line the
walls of the church):

> It was pretty ornery preaching—all about brotherly love and such-
> like tiresomeness; but everybody said it was a good sermon . . . and
> had a powerful lot to say about faith and good works and free grace
> and preforeordestination, and I don't know what all, that it did seem
> to me one of the roughest Sundays I had ever run across yet. [13:52]

Such a passage is profoundly Adamic because the humor it evokes
places Huck and the reader beyond the horror and necessity for
moral rage that the situation cries out for. We see that no reform is
possible for such people and that tragedy and comedy are inextric-
ably bound in a single moment. Yet we laugh, even though we
know that the tears will come when Buck is killed and the inevitable slaughter takes place. But the raft is waiting as Huck and Jim
float into the most Adamic episode of the book. In the famous sunrise passage, Huck's vernacular poetry reconciles all the contradictions in nature. As the sunrise beautifully unfolds, it reveals a
woodyard "piled by . . . cheats," while the breeze brings "sweet
smells" along with the smell of "dead fish laying around." The
blissful silence is balanced by the "bull-frogs a-cluttering," the
snags with the calm surface of the river, a white boy and black
man in naked racial harmony, with the "song birds just going it!"
(13:164). At night, Jim and Huck discuss their comically primitive
folk version of Genesis as they contemplate the origins of the stars,
either "made," as Jim says, or "just happened," as Huck believes.
They are momentarily free to mythologize and enjoy their prelap-
sarian experience.

Of course, the Duke and the King intrude upon this Eden, triggering a new series of adventures that culminate in the much vexed problem of Tom's "evasion" scheme, an extraordinary "daring jest" in itself. The outrageous comic paradox is that the full meaning of the book's Adamic conclusion comes from Tom, not Huck. For when Tom cries out the truth about Jim's being as "free as any cretur that walks this earth!" (13:399) and justifies setting free an already freed slave because of the *"adventure* of it" (13:400), he voices the triumph of its Adamic heroes over a satanic and confining "sivilization." And that is the essence of this kind of adventure story. The heroes are not in any fatal danger, not even Jim, though he comes the closest; for the happy end is prefigured in the beginning.

I see no moral lapse in the ending, complex as it is, but only shifting comic epiphanies because Tom, Huck, and Jim seek, for their different reasons, the possibilities of freedom-in-adventure, and not some abstract "truth." If the adventures in *Huckleberry Finn* are more threatening and varied than in *Tom Sawyer,* they are nevertheless cast in picaresque situations, demanding "freedom" from those moral struggles the adventures create. The "evasion" is but a final adventure that "providence" has granted to Tom and Huck, both of whom agree on the need for "style," as well as the destruction of conscience (13:321), in order to exploit the opportunity. They therefore wish not only to free Jim, in a burlesque fashion that parodies its own novel-adventure form and Dumas, but also to confound the Aunt Sallys and Uncle Silases of the adult world who would deny them that adventure. Their practical jokes, cruel as they are, end in teaching humility or reaffirming Jim's dignity and freedom, and are finally harmless compared to the reality of the townspeople's first impulse to hang Jim.

Given the novel's organic relationship between adventure and Adamic humor, we know that those characters who still seek the possibilities of life, whether in St. Petersburg or in the Territory, must be saved to do so. That is the novel's ethically positive content and its most affirmative comic reality. Its final theological jest is to escape the conflicting moralities of a fallen world and find new Edens, serpents and all. This is an Adamic comedy with a vengeance.

Now, with critical hindsight, we can see that *Huckleberry Finn* also marked the end of a phase in Mark Twain's career, insofar as it brought to a triumphant conclusion a nativist river epic begun with *Tom Sawyer* and carried forward by *Life on the Mississippi* (1883).[27] Viewed independently or as a trilogy, these works represent the "mythic" and most popular portion of the Mark Twain canon. They are also works in which Twain's countertheology had to confront and interpret the great river itself, as it flowed indifferently apart from man's spiritual struggles. As a "symbol of eternity" (12:235), as he calls it in *Life on the Mississippi*, the river, in its immutability, power, and beauty, literally and figuratively subsumes all those longings and issues with which he was engaged: childhood freedom, comic initiation into the ranks of the lordly pilots, personal guilt, and the force of technology destroying the "old" romance and poetry of nature. But when the river's attributes of eternal harmony and romantic possibility became "useless" to him, the satanic thrust of his countertheology, with its perverse providence, lies, and moral failure, begins to dominate. This is not to deny the obvious biographical facts of his many family and economic problems that contributed to his mood, but it is significant that, after *Huckleberry Finn*, he was never to return to his great symbol, once so vital to his imaginative life and public image. The causes are no doubt complex, but the satirical bite which in his earlier work gave such a sharp moral edge to his reputation as a genial entertainer, turns into the satanic laugh of hopelessness, the voice of Baudelaire's theological view of the humorist as the "Sage [who] laughs not save in fear and trembling,"[28] echoing Kierkegaard's insight. This laugh shatters the controlled tone of satirical anger, for its despair derives from losing faith in redeeming man from his fallen, reprobate condition, as well as from losing the sustaining spiritual balance the river had symbolized.

In *A Connecticut Yankee in King Arthur's Court* (1889), coming only a few years after *Huckleberry Finn*, this mode makes its comprehensive appearance. Often damned as a hodgepodge of tall-tale humor and French Revolutionary ideology, we can perhaps gain a fresh understanding of this "problematic"[29] book by concentrating on the way its comic modes embody Hank's changing perceptions about his hopes for revolution. For once he enters the "dream" world of Arthurian England, with its "wandering liars," and recognizes his chance for both personal power and radical change, the novel becomes a picaresque fantasy of a dream subverted by Hank's disturbing knowledge that not only is he "the wrong man" (14:171) to lead a Reign of Terror, but also that the effects of "training" will not yield in the end to his Tom Sawyer "effects," despite their spectacular successes.

This structural pattern cannot, by necessity, develop in a consistent tonal and linear progression, but must advance and retreat as Hank grapples with his incorrigible material. What is remarkable is the way the book's comic modes reflect this inconsistent process of moral surprise consistently. In Hank's contests with Merlin, his "shadow self," the humor is Adamically exultant, and arrogantly satisfied in its burlesque methods, fraught with hopes that a "new deal" will become a reality. But in his encounters with Morgan le Fay, in Sandy's embrace of the Nobility's "enchanted" hogs, in the degradation of the serfs, and finally through the Interdict itself, the revelations turn satanic, even scatological, in language and metaphor. The excrement the enchanted hogs leave becomes a "kind of Satire on Nature," Hank says. "It was the scientific method, the geologic method; it deposited the history of the family in a stratified record; and the antiquary could dig through it and tell by the remains what changes of diet that family had introduced successively for a hundred years" (14:182). And so to Hank's judgment of the human race as "muck" (14:430).

The wild burlesques that signaled Hank's joy at seeing the Old Order pass away are no longer possible, given this inevitable defeat by a totalitarian church. The Battle of the Sand-Belt, which ends with Merlin's deserved death and "petrified laugh" (14:447), negates satire itself, breaking through into calculated revenge. Hank tears up his plea to the knights to surrender in what appears to be a tragic parody of Huck's action. He gives his "mistimed sentimentalities a permanent rest" (14:438).

The book's comic epistemology has simultaneously exposed, affirmed, and denied humanity's "sentimentality," so we know it for what it is. This knowledge justifies Hank's despair about his life as "pathetic drift between eternities" (14:150), and so reinforces the epistemological doubts about how to distinguish between dream and reality, reaction and progress, which the final chapter overtly raises.

These doubts—and the satanic mood that permeates them—

arise from the novel's central theological thrust: Hank's American-Protestant revolution intrudes on a historical period whose God must necessarily resist its own destruction. The "Battle of the Sand Belt" embodies a clash between the God of the Old Order and the God of the New. Hank loses primarily because the theological time for his triumph has not yet come; the Reformation is still centuries away. It is Hank's triumph and tragedy to experience and suffer the consequences for attempting to change the course of history by himself. The rage in the book and Twain's insistence that reform or change can only come about through "force" show us how his "evangelical" stance had changed from the Adamic mood of *Huckleberry Finn*. Although Twain clearly affirms Hank's ideology over that of Medievalism, the satanic perspective springs not from Hank's personal failure, but from a mixture of Twain's rage and contempt at the apocalyptic nature of historical change.

This vision and the satanic laugh of extermination which accompanies it reach well into the "unkind laugh" of Young Satan (p. 137) as he describes the barbarous "progress" of humanity to Seppi and Theodor, and to the attitude of Huck, chief microbe liar in "Three Thousand Years among the Microbes," who longs to make a joke about the "old familiar rascals . . . in America" he has under his microscope. "I wanted to say, let's get that little speck out on a needle-point and make a gnat eat him, then give his remnants to his mother! But I didn't say it."[30] And it bursts into a holocaust-like pitch in "The United States of Lyncherdom" (1901, 1923) in his image of 203 blacks burning at the stake to light up the night and reveal the spires of five thousand churches. "O compassionate missionary, leave China! Come home and convert these Christians!" (29:248–49) is Twain's comic plea, the controlled irony of a preacher who knows how to image a present hell of racial extermination for a congregation of a million cowardly persons. The technique may be derived from Swift, but in Twain the ironic voice is not emotionally detached from the horror it confronts; rather, it contains the palpable laugh of a satanic ironist whose only solution is to enlist "martial personalities," like the "Merrills and Beloats," in order to humiliate the exterminators. This is but another facet of the negative content of the preacher's countertheology and the variety of "daring jests" it could generate.

The only positive qualification to these otherwise satanically "daring jests" is that the artist, whether in the guise of an exiled Satan, "The Bishop of New Jersey," or a "Mad Philosopher," continues to create or preach, reminding his reprobates of their imperialism and money lust. At the same time, he offers them—and himself—the dubious consolation that the whole tragic farce is God's responsibility.[31]

I have argued that Mark Twain's countertheology and its comic modes are rooted in an epistemological method which gives it its unique force and originality, and from which criticism might well take its starting point in reassessing his comedy. It is certainly as profound or complex a method as, for example, Cervantes', who juxtaposes the "God idea" of his knight's mad imagination—his *ingenioso*—with Sancho's common sense or *discreto*, the two comically modifying each other's way of perceiving the nature of reality through the adventures their clash helps create.[32] From this comic epistemological base, Cervantes is able to produce a myriad of burlesque and satirical situations which can only be resolved with Quixote's "return" to sanity and a normative Christian death.

In Mark Twain, humor springs from and acts as a mediating power between an Adamic adventurer who juxtaposes both his "God idea" and frontier democratic values against the world's inherent social and religious contradictions, thus creating new knowledge of that fallen reality in every fresh encounter.[33] The process reaches its inevitable end when it is no longer possible to affirm, through that humor, the possibilities of moral change and a coherent universe. The satanic laughter emerges in full force only when this final revelation is acknowledged in all its absurd manifestations.

Yet, each revelation must effect a corresponding critical shift in the reader's perception of what new "truth" the preacher-artist's "God idea" or countertheology dramatizes. By its very nature, Mark Twain's comic vision demands from the critic an Emersonian inconsistency. The social problem was that Twain's Lincolnian and public, self-created images embodied forms of familiar comic patterns, whereas the preacher's art and jests were consistently inconsistent, uncomfortably disrupting his "normal" social themes, such as childhood, democracy, the "self," and historical progress. Twain's comic epistemology penetrated so deeply into his social and personal themes that it finally achieved a vast satanic perspective. And only from that angle of vision can we measure the progress and power of the myth of his "daring jest" in world comic literature.

It all sprang from one driving impulse: the need for Mark Twain to use his "profane instincts" and, like Huck Finn, lie his way into the "sacred bounds" in order to assert his true identity at last. If this be mythology, let us make the most of it.

Notes

Introduction (Davis)

1. "The Literary Remains of Mark Twain," *Virginia Quarterly Review*, 53 (1977), 353–62.
2. *Democracy in America*, the Henry Reeve text as revised by Francis Bowen (New York: Random House, 1945), 2:63.
3. *Democracy and the Novel: Popular Resistance to Classic American Writers* (New York: Oxford University Press, 1978).
4. *Mr. Clemens and Mark Twain* (New York: Simon and Schuster, 1966), p. 361.
5. As quoted in ibid., p. 358.
6. de Tocqueville, *Democracy in America*, p. 43.
7. "Mark Twain and His Times: A Bicentennial Appreciation," *SAQ*, 76 (1977), 133–46. Pettit notes that his titles are in fact taken from a standard text of American history.
8. *Mark Twain's Notebooks: Prepared for Publication with Comments by Albert Bigelow Paine* (New York: Harper's, 1935), p. 372.
9. Professor Helmbrecht Breinig has been kind enough to share (in a letter to me) some of his recent work on Twain. *Satire und Roman*, his forthcoming book on the satirical novel in American literature, includes a major component on Twain.
10. "Our Best Political Novel," *New York Times Book Review*, 6 June 1976, p. 1.
11. See *American Literary Realism*, 12 (1979), 343–46.
12. Two major publishing projects under way simultaneously at the University of California, Berkeley, are *The Papers of Mark Twain* (which

includes letters, notebooks, journals, etc.) and *The Works of Mark Twain*. In the past 15 years, the following books have examined various aspects of Twain's life and/or extraliterary writings: Dewey Ganzel, *Mark Twain Abroad: The Cruise of the "Quaker City"* (Chicago and London: University of Chicago Press, 1968); Fred Lorch, *The Trouble Begins at Eight: Mark Twain's Lecture Tours* (Ames: Iowa State University Press, 1968); Edgar Branch, ed., *Clemens of the "Call": Mark Twain in San Francisco* (Berkeley: University of California Press, 1969); Arthur Scott, *Mark Twain at Large* (Chicago: Henry Regnery Co., 1969); Howard Baetzhold, *Mark Twain and John Bull* (Bloomington and London: Indiana University Press, 1970); Earl J. Dias, ed., *Mark Twain's Letters to the Rogers Family* (New Bedford, Mass.: Reynolds-DeWalt Printing, 1970); Hamlin Hill, *Mark Twain: God's Fool* (New York: Harper & Row, 1973); Paul Fatout, ed., *Mark Twain Speaking* (Iowa City: University of Iowa Press, 1976); Louis Budd, ed., *A Listing and Selection from Newspaper and Magazine Interviews of Samuel Clemens: 1874–1910* (Arlington, Tex.: American Literary Realism, 1977); Paul Fatout, ed., *Mark Twain Speaks for Himself* (West Lafayette, Ind.: Purdue University Press, 1978); William R. Macnaughton, *Mark Twain's Last Years as a Writer* (Columbia: University of Missouri Press, 1979).

Collecting the Works of Mark Twain (Gerber)

1. *Book Collector's Market*, 4, no. 4 (July/August 1879), 1.
2. Ibid., p. 9.
3. *Bibliography of American Literature* (New Haven: Yale University Press, 1957), 2:173–234.
4. *Mark Twain: A Reference Guide* (Boston: G. K. Hall, 1977). Six supplements have appeared in *American Literary Realism: 1870– 1910*, usually in the autumn issue.
5. *Book Collector's Handbook of Values* (1982–83 ed.) (New York: G. P. Putnam's Sons, 1982), pp. 580–84.
6. *ABC for Book Collectors* (New York: Knopf, 1976), pp. 97–99.

"Norman Rockwell Sentimentality" (Ensor)

1. (Boston: G. K. Hall, 1980), p. xii.
2. (New York: Watson-Guptill, 1979), p. 9.
3. (New York: Watson-Guptill, 1946), pp. 101–07. Hereafter cited as Guptill.

4. (Garden City, N.Y.: Doubleday, 1960), pp. 302–06. Hereafter cited as Rockwell.

5. E. W. Kemble, "Illustrating Huck Finn," *Colophon* (1930), part 1, article 5.

6. Rockwell, p. 303.

7. Ibid., p. 306.

8. Guptill, p. 101.

9. Ibid., p. 107.

10. Ibid.

11. Rockwell, pp. 305–06.

12. Ibid., p. 306.

13. *Tom Sawyer*, chap. 2. I would like to thank MBI for their generous permission to reprint The Heritage Club illustrations.

14. Ibid., chap. 28.

15. *The Adventures of Tom Sawyer, Tom Sawyer Abroad, Tom Sawyer, Detective*, ed. John C. Gerber, Paul Baender, and Terry Firkins (Berkeley: University of California Press, 1980), pp. 471, 562.

16. Rockwell, p. 302.

17. *Tom Sawyer*, chap. 6. All my quotations are from the California edition cited above. The passage is quoted in Rockwell, p. 305.

18. Guptill, p. 105.

19. This illustration appears in *Rockwell on Rockwell*, p. 71.

20. *Rockwell on Rockwell*, p. 86.

21. *Tom Sawyer*, chap. 9.

22. I am indebted to Professor Marcia Jacobson of Auburn University for making this point clearer to me than it previously had been.

23. *Rockwell on Rockwell*, p. 86.

24. Guptill, p. 100.

25. Ibid., p. 103.

26. *Green Hills of Africa* (New York: Scribner's, 1935), p. 22. Hemingway may have had in mind the 1931 film version in which Tom Sawyer (played by Jackie Coogan) does indeed accompany Huck and Jim down the river on a raft.

27. Rockwell, p. 304.

28. *Tom Sawyer*, chap. 31.

29. Guptill, p. 103.

30. Rockwell, p. 304.

31. Ibid., p. 303.

32. *Huckleberry Finn*, chap. 5. All my quotations are from the first American edition of the novel.

33. Cf. Matt. 6:6 (KJV): "When thou prayest, enter into thy closet."

34. *Huckleberry Finn*, chap. 10.
35. Ibid., chap. 19.
36. Ibid., chap. 25.
37. Ibid., chap. 28.
38. Ibid., chap. 19.
39. Heritage Club, *Sandglass*, no. 4D-R, p. 4. This leaflet is sent to members who receive the *Huckleberry Finn* volume from the club.
40. A double-page advertisement in the *New York Review of Books* (21 January 1982, pp. 4–5) mentions the Twain volumes and how the "warm and witty Rockwell" captured "the mischief of Tom and Huck in their meanderings along Twain's beloved Mississippi River." The same advertisement appeared in *Life* and other popular magazines.
41. *Rockwell on Rockwell*, p. 16.
42. Heritage Club, *Sandglass*, no. 3A-R, p. 2. This leaflet is sent to members who receive the *Tom Sawyer* volume from the club.

Autobiography as Property (Gribben)

1. "Mark Twain Himself," *Sewanee Review*, 83 (Fall 1975), 708.
2. *Life and Lillian Gish* (New York: Macmillan, 1932), pp. 277–78.
3. See Louis J. Budd's "A Listing of and Selection from Newspaper and Magazine Interviews with Samuel L. Clemens, 1874–1910," *American Literary Realism*, 10 (Winter 1977), 1–100.
4. Clemens to William Wright, Hartford, 29 March 1875, ALS in the Mark Twain Project, Bancroft Library, University of California, Berkeley. I am grateful to Robert H. Hirst, editor, for access to this collection and for helpful suggestions.
5. *Mark Twain, Business Man*, ed. Samuel C. Webster (Boston: Little, Brown, 1946), p. 389.
6. Quoted by Lord Birkenhead in *Rudyard Kipling* (New York: Random House, 1978), p. 343. Kipling's letter was dated 6 October 1932.
7. *Mark Twain's Correspondence with Henry Huttleston Rogers*, ed. Lewis Leary (Berkeley: University of California Press, 1969), p. 477, n. 2.—hereafter cited as *MTHHR*. My italics added in this quotation.
8. "Authorship and Craft: The Example of Mark Twain," *Southern Review*, 12 (April 1976), 247–48.
9. Thomas Marc Parrott, "Mark Twain: Made in America," *Booklover's Magazine*, 3 (February 1904), 145–54; reprinted in *Mark Twain: The Critical Heritage*, ed. Frederick Anderson (New York: Barnes & Noble, 1971), quotations from pp. 244, 249.

10. *Mark Twain's Letters to His Publishers*, ed. Hamlin Hill (Berkeley: University of California Press, 1967), pp. 42–43—hereafter cited as *MTLP*.

11. Ibid., p. 48.

12. Ibid., pp. 56 (n. 2), 112, 116.

13. *Mark Twain's Autobiography*, ed. Albert Bigelow Paine, 2 vols. (New York: Harper & Brothers, 1924), 1:288.

14. Henry Adams to Henry James, Paris, 6 May 1908, *Letters of Henry Adams*, ed. Worthington Chauncey Ford, 2 vols. (Boston: Houghton Mifflin, 1938), 2:495.

15. *Mark Twain in Eruption,* ed. Bernard DeVoto (New York: Harper & Brothers, 1940), p. 340.

16. Quoted by Gerald Langford, *Alias O. Henry: A Biography of William Sidney Porter* (New York: Macmillan, 1957), p. 231.

17. *Mark Twain–Howells Letters*, ed. Henry Nash Smith and William M. Gibson (Cambridge, Mass.: Harvard University Press, Belknap Press, 1960), p. 781.

18. *Mark Twain: A Biography* (New York: Harper & Brothers, 1912), pp. 1269, 1267.

19. *The Ordeal of Mark Twain*, rev. ed. (New York: E. P. Dutton & Co., 1933), p. 17.

20. *My Father, Mark Twain* (New York: Harper & Brothers, 1931), pp. 268, 265.

21. Ibid., p. 290.

22. *Mark Twain and His World* (London: Michael Joseph, 1974), pp. 11, 93.

Mark Twain, "Funniest Man in the World" (Smith)

1. The phrase "Funniest Man in the World" appears in a subheading in the New York *Journal & Advertiser*, "American Magazine Supplement," 11 November 1900, p. 18. A writer signing himself "Becket" declared in the Liverpool *Post* (24 June 1907): "There is little doubt that the most humorous man the world has ever known is Samuel Langhorne Clemens" (clipping in Scrapbook 31, p. [49], compiled by Clemens' secretary, Ralph W. Ashcroft; in Mark Twain Papers, The Bancroft Library, University of California, Berkeley).

2. A London *Morning Leader* (21 June 1907) clipping (in Scrapbook 32, p. [16]), called Mark Twain "doubtless the most successful and famous man of our time." In 1909 Archibald Henderson declared in *Harper's*

Monthly that "his name is more widely known than that of any other living man" (repr. in Arthur L. Scott, ed., *Mark Twain: Selected Criticism* [Dallas: Southern Methodist University Press, 1955], p. 99).

3. Louis J. Budd, ed., *A Listing of and Selection from Newspaper and Magazine Interviews with Samuel L. Clemens, 1874–1910* (Arlington, Tex.: University of Texas at Arlington, 1977); Fred W. Lorch, *The Trouble Begins at Eight: Mark Twain's Lecture Tours* (Ames: Iowa State University Press, 1968); Paul Fatout, *Mark Twain on the Lecture Circuit* (Bloomington: Indiana University Press, 1960); Paul Fatout, *Mark Twain in Virginia City* (Bloomington: Indiana University Press, 1964); Edgar M. Branch, ed., *Clemens of the* Call*: Mark Twain in San Francisco* (Berkeley: University of California Press, 1969); Robert M. Rodney, "Mark Twain in England. A Study of the English Criticism of and Attitude toward Mark Twain: 1867–1940" (unpub. diss., University of Wisconsin, 1945); Howard G. Baetzhold, *Mark Twain and John Bull: The British Connection* (Bloomington: Indiana University Press, 1970); Dennis Welland, *Mark Twain in England* (London: Chatto and Windus, 1978).

4. Lowell, *Complete Writings*, 16 vols. (Cambridge, Mass.: Riverside Press, 1904), 11:10, 8.

5. Sydney Mendel, "A Note on Lowell's 'Ode Recited at the Harvard Commemoration,'" *New England Quarterly*, 35 (March 1962), 102–03. Henry James observed, in an essay in the *Atlantic* in 1892, that some of Lowell's poetry was "too literary. . . . One feels at moments that he speaks in verse mainly because he is penetrated with what verse has achieved" (*Atlantic*, 69 [January 1892], 43–44; quoted by Mendel, p. 103).

6. *Bits of Gossip* (Westminster: Archibald Constable, 1904), pp. 42–43.

7. Henry N. Smith, "That Hideous Mistake of Poor Clemens's," *Harvard Library Bulletin*, 9 (Spring 1955), 145–80.

8. Brander Matthews declared in 1897 that upon the publication of "The Notorious Jumping Frog" and *Innocents Abroad*, Mark Twain was "classified promptly as a professional humorist" by "the average public opinion"—as "a writer whose sole duty it was to make us laugh, and to whom therefore we need never give a second thought after the smile had faded from our faces" ("Mark Twain—His Work," *Book–Buyer*, 13 [January 1897], 977).

9. *My Dear Bro.: A Letter from Samuel Clemens to his Brother Orion*, ed. Frederick Anderson (Berkeley: The Berkeley Albion, 1961), p. 6.

10. SLC to Mary Fairbanks, Elmira, N.Y., 6 January 1869: "Anybody who could convince her [Olivia Langdon] that I was not a humorist would secure her eternal gratitude! She thinks a humorist is something perfectly

awful" (Dixon Wecter, ed., *Mark Twain to Mrs. Fairbanks* [San Marino, Calif.: Huntington Library, 1949], p. 63).

11. Fatout, *Mark Twain on the Lecture Circuit*, p. 40.

12. Josiah G. Holland, editor of *Scribner's Monthly* and probably the most sought after lyceum lecturer of the pompous, conventional type, attacked the increasingly popular comic speakers in his magazine (February 1872) as "Triflers on the Platform" and "literary buffoons." He charged that the humorists "disseminated slang and vitiated the taste of the impressible" (quoted in Fatout, *Mark Twain on the Lecture Circuit*, p. 142). Mark Twain composed a reply to Holland, "An Appeal from One That Is Persecuted," but did not publish it (DV 125, TS in Mark Twain Papers).

13. Fatout, *Mark Twain on the Lecture Circuit*, p. 136.

14. Henry N. Smith, *Mark Twain: The Development of a Writer* (Cambridge, Mass.: Belknap Press of Harvard University Press, 1962), pp. 106–07; cf. also John H. Raleigh, *Matthew Arnold and American Culture* (Berkeley: University of California Press, 1957), pp. 64–65.

15. Jacob G. Schurman, president of Cornell University, quoted in San Francisco *Call* ("Likens Twain to Lincoln," 24 April 1910, p. 22). Howells used the phrase as a climax to the series of reminiscences published in *Harper's Monthly* (July–September 1910), and issued as a book later that year under the title *My Mark Twain*.

16. New York *American & Journal*, 26 November 1905, quoted in Charles Neider, ed., *Mark Twain: Life as I Find It* (Garden City, N.Y.: Hanover House, 1961), p. 377.

17. New York *Times*, 6 December 1905, p. 1.

18. "Mark Twain's 70th Birthday. Souvenir of Its Celebration," Supplement to *Harper's Weekly*, 45 (23 December 1905), 1886. Subsequent citations within parentheses in the text.

19. Author of such best-sellers as *Rebecca of Sunnybrook Farm* (1903), which she signed with the name Kate Douglas Wiggin (from a former marriage).

20. "On the Psychology of the Trickster Figure," in Paul Radin, *The Trickster: A Study in American Indian Mythology*, with commentaries by Karl Kerényi and C. G. Jung (New York: Schocken, 1956), p. 209. Subsequent citations within parentheses in the text.

21. Clemens ascribes this theological "disease" to Mollie Clemens, wife of his brother Orion, in a letter to Howells (Munich, 9 February 1879; *Mark Twain–Howells Letters*, ed. Henry N. Smith and William M. Gibson, 2 vols. [Cambridge, Mass.: Belknap Press of Harvard University Press, 1960], 1:256).

22. St. Louis *Republican*, 24 March 1867, quoted in Fatout, *Mark Twain on the Lecture Circuit*, p. 30.

23. Henry N. Smith, ed., *Mark Twain of the "Enterprise"* (Berkeley: University of California Press, 1957), p. 21.

24. Fatout, *Mark Twain on the Lecture Circuit*, p. 54.

25. Ibid., p. 52.

26. Ibid., pp. 237–38.

27. Alfred M. Lee, *The Daily Newspaper in America: The Evolution of a Social Instrument* (New York: Macmillan, 1937), p. 435. In 1883 the largest-circulation daily papers in New York City were as follows:

	Daily	Sunday
Sun	145,000	152,000
Herald	135,000	_____
Tribune	50,000	55,000
Morning Journal	100,000	_____
World	59,000	60,000

In 1903 the figures were as follows:

Evening Journal	600,000	_____
American & Journal	300,000	700,000
World	250,000	450,000
Herald	130,000	245,000
Sun	120,000	150,000
Times	100,000	_____

(Statistics from *N. W. Ayer & Son's American Newspaper Annual*, Philadelphia, 1884 and 1903).

28. Chicago, 1940, esp. chap. 8, pp. 184–216.

29. Nils Gunnar Nilsson, "The Origins of the Interview," *Journalism Quarterly*, 48 (Winter 1971), 707–13; Lee, *Daily Newspaper*, pp. 616–17.

30. London *Daily Express*, 19 June 1907, clipping in Scrapbook 31, p. [7].

31. London *Daily News*, 26 June 1907, clipping in Scrapbook 31, p. [56]. In another interview, Clemens revived a comic fantasy from the *Burlesque Autobiography* that he had published in 1871 (and then suppressed) by saying: "The Twain family . . . had in the ancient time busily engaged in the industries of murder and assassination. But lately they had been going in merely for unostentatious burglary and theft, because they were becoming noticeable" (London *Evening News*, 18 June 1907; clipping in Scrapbook 31, p. [4]).

32. London *Star*, 26 June 1907, clipping in Scrapbook 32, p. [53].

33. New York *Sun*, 23 July 1907, repr. in Budd, ed., *Interviews*, p. 91.

34. New York *Times*, 23 July 1907, repr. in Neider, ed., *Life as I Find It*, p. 395.

35. London *Daily Mail*, 19 June 1907, clipping in Scrapbook 32, p. [5].

36. *Blackwood's Magazine*, August 1907, repr. in Frederick Anderson, ed., *Mark Twain: The Critical Heritage* (New York: Barnes & Noble, 1971), p. 271. Eliot's obituary essay on Whibley, published in 1931, is the concluding item in *Selected Essays 1917–1936* (New York, 1932), pp. 403–15.

37. Arnold's reactions to the United States on the basis of his lecture tour in 1883 are discussed by Howard Mumford Jones in "Arnold, Aristocracy, and America," *American Historical Review*, 49 (April 1944), 393–409.

38. *Critical Heritage*, pp. 275–76.

39. London *Daily Chronicle*, 19 June 1907, clipping in Scrapbook 32, p. [13].

40. London *Daily Telegraph*, 26 June 1907, clipping in Scrapbook 32, p. [48].

41. SLC to Howells, Elmira, 24 August 1889. It may be significant that the reason he gives for his decision is, "I'm not writing for those parties who miscall themselves critics, & I don't care to have them paw the book at all" (*Mark Twain–Howells Letters*, 2:610–11).

42. Hartford, 22 September 1889, in *Mark Twain–Howells Letters*, 2:613.

43. "Mark Twain's Bequest," London *Times*, 23 May 1899, repr. in Budd, ed., *Interviews*, p.80.

44. Dublin, N.H., 17 June 1906, and New York, 26 June 1906, in *Mark Twain–Howells Letters*, 2:811, 815.

45. "Mark the Double Twain," *English Journal*, 24 (October 1935), 616, repr. in Lewis Leary, ed., *A Casebook on Mark Twain's Wound* (New York: Cromwell, 1962), p. 146.

46. New York, 1 August 1926, quoted in *Mark Twain: God's Fool*, p. 268.

47. Unsigned article, *The Spectator* (London), 104 (30 April 1910), 721.

48. William M. Gibson, "Introduction," *Mark Twain's Mysterious Stranger Manuscripts* (Berkeley: University of California Press, 1969), p. 4.

49. *Mark Twain's Autobiography*, ed. Albert B. Paine, 2 vols. (New York: Harper & Brothers, 1924); *The Autobiography of Mark Twain*, ed. Charles Neider (New York: Harper & Brothers, 1959).

50. The most thorough discussion of the composition of the autobio-

graphical dictation is Renate Schmidt-von Bardeleben, *Studien zur amerikanischen Autobiographie: Benjamin Franklin und Mark Twain* (Munich, 1981).

51. "All modern American literature comes from one book by Mark Twain called *Huckleberry Finn*. If you read it you must stop where the Nigger Jim is stolen from the boys. That is the real end. The rest is just cheating. But it's the best book we've had. There was nothing before. There has been nothing as good since." *Green Hills of Africa* (New York: Scribner's, 1935), p. 22.

52. Neil Schmitz, *Of Huck and Alice: Humorous Writing in American Literature* (Minneapolis: University of Minnesota Press, 1983).

A "Talent for Posturing" (Budd)

1. *The Works of Mark Twain: Early Tales & Sketches, Vol. 1, 1851–1864*, eds. Edgar M. Branch and Robert H. Hirst (Berkeley: University of California Press, 1980), 15:185. Briefly, Martin Greene applies the larger tradition to Twain in *Re-Appraisals: Some Commonsense Readings in American Literature* (New York: Norton, 1964), pp. 113–16; the point runs incidentally throughout David E. E. Sloane, *Mark Twain as a Literary Comedian* (Baton Rouge: Louisiana State University Press, 1979). Also relevant is Dennis B. Downey, "George Francis Train: The Great American Humbug," *Journal of Popular Culture*, 14 (Fall 1980), 251–61.

2. E. M. Branch, "Introduction," *Early Tales & Sketches*, pp. 16, 24, 53–54.

3. Henry Mills Alden, "Mark Twain: Personal Impressions," *Book News Monthly*, 28 (April 1910), 579, 581.

4. Boston *Herald*, 6 November 1905, p. 4; Baltimore *Sun*, 12 May 1907, p. 20.

5. See Louis J. Budd, "Color Him Curious about Yellow Journalism: Mark Twain and the New York City Press," *Journal of Popular Culture*, 15 (Fall 1981), 25–33.

6. Carlyle Smythe, "The Real 'Mark Twain,'" *Pall Mall Magazine*, 16 (September 1898), 31.

7. Interview in Pittsburgh *Chronicle Telegraph*, 29 December 1884, p. 1.

8. Quoted in Justin Kaplan, *Mr. Clemens and Mark Twain* (New York: Simon and Schuster, 1966), p. 33.

9. "I Rise to a Question of Privilege," holograph manuscript in Vassar College Library; written in 1868.

10. Dixon Wecter, ed., *Mark Twain to Mrs. Fairbanks* (San Marino, Calif.: Huntington Library, 1949), p. 153.

11. (New York) *Bookman,* 13 (July 1901), 415.

12. *Mark Twain's Autobiography,* ed. Albert Bigelow Paine, 2 vols. (New York: Harper Brothers, 1924), 2:312.

13. See the New York *World, Sun, Times,* and *Tribune* of 15 April 1906 for slightly differing versions. However, Twain spoke to the reporters from prepared notes.

14. "Mark Twain as Our Emissary," *Century Magazine,* 81 (December 1910), 204. After this beginning, Ade shrewdly and wittily analyzed Twain's popularity; while doing so, he testified to its strength.

15. Paul Fatout, ed., *Mark Twain Speaking* (Iowa City: University of Iowa Press, 1976), has an almost complete listing and reconstructs most of the texts.

16. In DV 131 (MTP); not published, so far as I can find; it should be dated December 1887 or January 1888. Previously unpublished materials by Mark Twain are © 1981 by Edward J. Willi and Manufacturers Hanover Trust Company as trustees of the Mark Twain Foundation, and are published with the permission of the University of California Press and Robert H. Hirst, general editor of the Mark Twain Project in Berkeley, California.

17. *Walt Whitman: A Life* (New York: Simon and Schuster, 1980), p. 38.

18. By now I can add twenty items to my *Listing of and Selection from Newspaper and Magazine Interviews with Samuel L. Clemens* (Arlington, Tex.: ALR Press, 1977—also as vol. 10, no. 1 of *American Literary Realism, 1870–1910*).

19. Quoted in Giuseppe Gadda Conti, "L'America Nel 'Corriere' e Nella 'Stampa': Mark Twain," *Studi Americani,* 19–20 (1973–74), 147.

Life on the Mississippi Revisited (Cox)

1. See my *Mark Twain: The Fate of Humor* (Princeton: Princeton University Press, 1966), pp. 105–26, 161–67.

2. The most penetrating and suggestive treatments of this passage that I know are by Henry Nash Smith, *Mark Twain: The Development of a Writer* (Cambridge, Mass.: Harvard University Press, 1962), pp. 77–81, and Larzer Ziff, "Authorship and Craft: The Example of Mark Twain," *Southern Review,* 12 n.s. (1976), 256–60.

3. For interesting discussions relating the art of piloting to the art of writing, see Edgar J. Burde, "Mark Twain: The Writer as Pilot," *PMLA* 93

(1978), 878–92; Sherwood Cummings, "Mark Twain's Theory of Realism; or the Science of Piloting," *Studies in American Humor,* 2 (1976), 209–21; and Larzer Ziff, "Authorship and Craft," 246–60.

4. Anyone interested in the conception, composition, and interpretation of *Life on the Mississippi* will find Horst H. Kruse's *Mark Twain and "Life on the Mississippi"* (Amherst: University of Massachusetts Press, 1981) indispensable. For a briefer account which corrects many prior errors and misconceptions concerning the composition of *Life on the Mississippi,* see Guy A. Cardwell, "Life on the Mississippi: Vulgar Facts and Learned Errors," *Emerson Society Quarterly,* 46 (1973), 283–93.

5. Walter Blair's "When Was *Huckleberry Finn* Written?" *American Literature,* 30 (1958), 1–20, remains the most succinct and authoritative effort to establish the chronology of composition of *Huckleberry Finn.* For the full account of Mark Twain's composition of *Life on the Mississippi* during the summer of 1882, see Kruse, pp. 43–91.

6. I use the Author's National Edition because it is the text most readily available in libraries to the general reader.

7. For a thorough account of this issue, see Peter D. Beidler, "The Raft Episode in *Huckleberry Finn,*" *Modern Fiction Studies,* 14 (Spring 1968), 11–20.

8. But contenders for a serious reading will have to contend with the fact that Mark Twain repeats the claim that the Mississippi drains Delaware: "A few more days swept swiftly by, and La Salle stood in the shadow of his confiscating cross, at a meeting of the waters from Delaware, and from Itasca, and from the mountain ranges close upon the Pacific, with the waters of the Gulf of Mexico, his task finished, his prodigy achieved (*Life on the Mississippi,* Author's National Edition, p. 16). I suppose it would be possible to argue that Mark Twain was so stupid that he didn't know that the Mississippi *doesn't* drain Delaware!

9. Stanley Brodwin's "The Useful and Useless River: *Life on the Mississippi* Revisited," *Studies in American Humor,* 2 (1976), 196–208, is a splendid interpretation of the structure and meaning of the continuity, as well as the discontinuity, of these episodes.

10. Because of Mark Twain's notorious penchant for unreliability, the scholarship devoted to his account of acquiring his pen name is necessarily extensive. The most authoritative treatment of this episode, at once summarizing and correcting prior scholarship, is in Kruse, pp. 82–90.

11. Samuel Clemens' first known use of "Mark Twain" occurred on 3 February 1863 in the Virginia City *Territorial Enterprise,* well before he left Nevada for California.

12. There was an earlier occasion when Nixon became the unwitting victim of his own speech. In the campaign of 1960 he repeatedly told

the nation, "We can't stand pat," presumably forgetting that his wife's name was Pat—or is it possible that he was the victim of a malicious speechwriter?

Mark Twain and the Myth of the West (Kolb)

1. Joseph Campbell, *The Hero with a Thousand Faces* (Princeton: Princeton University Press, 1949, 1968), p. 3.

2. (Garden City, N.Y.: Doubleday, 1952), pp. 82–83. The theory of the West's difference is of course dominated by Frederick Jackson Turner, who began his campaign with "The Significance of the Frontier in American History," an essay read to the American Historical Association at the Chicago Columbian Exposition in 1893. A 92-item bibliography of "The Frontier Hypothesis and Frederick Jackson Turner" is contained in *The Frontier and the American West*, comp. R. W. Paul and R. E. Etulain (Arlington Heights, Ill.: AHM Publishing Corp., 1977).

3. *The Great Plains* (Boston: Ginn and Co., 1931; rpt. New York: Grosset & Dunlap, n.d.), p. 9. In *A Natural History of Western Trees* (Boston: Houghton Mifflin, 1953), Donald Culross Peattie states that the 100th meridian is a botanical line of demarcation: "There are only about twenty species, out of more than two hundred, which cross this boundary between the western and the [northeastern] sylvas, and approximately the same number, though quite a different lot of species, do so in Texas where the western and southeastern floras just meet on the almost treeless plains" (p. xii).

4. Published in volume 8—*Tales, Sketches, and Reports*—of the University of Virginia edition of *The Works of Stephen Crane* (Charlottesville: University Press of Virginia, 1973), p. 474. Crane's spelling is "trays."

5. *Original Journals of the Lewis and Clark Expedition* (New York: Dodd, Mead and Co., 1904), 2:153–54. Lewis spells it "beatifull." Jefferson, *Notes on the State of Virginia* (New York: Harper & Row, 1964), p. 21.

6. The quotation from Byrd is contained in George R. Stewart, *Names on the Land* (New York: Random House, 1945), p. 128. My identification of Byrd's Buffalo Creek with present-day Buffalo Springs (called Buffalo Junction in some atlases) is a conjecture based on its location: 155 miles inland, 7 miles north of the present Virginia–North Carolina boundary. Buffalo Lick was the original name of the site on the north fork of the Yadkin River settled by Squire Boone and his family, including young Daniel, in 1751. In addition to the locations cited in the text, there is a Buffalo Gap, Virginia; a Buffalo, Tennessee; and another Buffalo, Kentucky.

7. *The Far Western Frontier* (New York: Harper & Row, 1956, 1962), p. 44.

8. New York City, etc.: the birthplaces, respectively, of William James, John Dewey, and Charles S. Peirce.

9. *Frontier: American Literature and the American West* (Princeton: Princeton University Press, 1965, 1970), p. 13.

10. *Specimen Days*, in *Leaves of Grass and Selected Prose* (New York: Random House, 1950), pp. 705, 711, 713.

11. "Galveston, Texas," p. 474.

12. Arthur Chapman, *Out Where the West Begins and Other Western Verses* (Boston: Houghton Mifflin, 1917), p. 1.

13. *Democracy in America*, 2 vols., ed. Phillips Bradley (New York: Random House, 1945), 1:59. See also appendix H (2:370–71), which summarizes "qualifications of voters in the United States." Billington, *The Far Western Frontier* (pp. 99–100), describes the lawmaking of the Overland pioneers.

14. *The American Commonwealth*, rev. ed. (New York: Macmillan, 1919), 1:892. Bryce also suggests the concept of difference: "There has been nothing in the past resembling its growth, and probably there will be nothing in the future. A vast territory, wonderfully rich in natural resources of many kinds . . . in many places marvellously fertile; in some regions mountains full of minerals, in others trackless forests where every tree is over two hundred feet high . . . these are phenomena absolutely without precedent in history."

15. *Songs of the West* (Columbia record CL659).

16. Henry Nash Smith, *Virgin Land* (Cambridge, Mass.: Harvard University Press, 1950).

17. *The Principles of Psychology*, 2 vols. (New York: Henry Holt and Co., 1890; Dover ed. 1950), 2:103.

18. William Bradford, *Of Plymouth Plantation*, in *The American Puritans*, ed. Perry Miller (Garden City, N.Y.: Doubleday, 1956), p. 17.

19. Peattie, *A Natural History of Western Trees*: "[Lodgepole] seed life, sealed between the scales by a heavy coat of stiff resin, is not killed by . . . fire. Indeed, the resin is melted, the cones are roasted till their scales pop open, and out leaps the seed crop that has been dormant for years" (p. 104). See the USDA "Revised Fire Management Policy" (Washington: Department of Agriculture, n.d., effective February 1978).

20. Robert Graves, *The White Goddess* (New York: Creative Age Press, 1948); Northrup Frye, *The Educated Imagination* (Bloomington: Indiana University Press, 1964), pp. 111, 52, 55.

21. I have used the Robert Fitzgerald translation of lines 26–27, book 5, *The Odyssey* (Garden City, N.Y.: Doubleday, 1961). Odysseus' endear-

ing mixture of morality and skeptical pragmatism leads right to Huck Finn: "So I reckoned I wouldn't bother no more about it, but after this always do whichever come handiest at the time." *Adventures of Huckleberry Finn* (New York: Charles L. Webster and Co., 1885), p. 128.

22. John William Ward's much reprinted "The Meaning of Lindbergh's Flight" first appeared in *American Quarterly*, vol. 10 (Spring 1958). In that essay, Ward suggests that these two ideas are exclusive: "The response to Lindbergh reveals that the American people were deeply torn between conflicting interpretations of their own experience. . . . Whether we can have both the freedom of the individual and the power of an organized society is a question that still haunts our minds. To resolve that conflict . . . is still the task of America." In a later essay, reworking the same ground, Ward moves toward a more complex analysis: "In Lindbergh's case, two different evaluations are involved and, analytically, they are irreconcilable; if we run either interpretation to its logical conclusion, it negates the other. But I doubt if any society has a single, coherent, one-dimensional system of values; there is always a tension, a potential polarity, between opposing ideals. A definition of reality as a field of tensions between poles which define each other seems closer, at least, to my own experience than the frame of mind which says it has to be one or the other." *Carlton Miscellany*, 6 (Summer 1965), 38.

23. *Altgeld's America: The Lincoln Ideal versus Changing Realities* (New York: Funk & Wagnalls, 1958; New York: Franklin Watts, 1973), p. 7.

24. *Roughing It*. All quotations are from the CEAA edition, edited by Franklin R. Rogers and Paul Baender (Berkeley: University of California Press, 1972). Henry Nash Smith has provided our most influential discussion of *Roughing It* in "Mark Twain as an Interpreter of the Far West: The Structure of *Roughing It*" in *The Frontier in Perspective*, ed. W. D. Wyman and C. B. Kroeber (Madison: University of Wisconsin Press, 1956), revised into "Transformation of a Tenderfoot," chap. 3 of *Mark Twain: The Development of a Writer* (Cambridge, Mass.: Harvard University Press, 1962). Professor Smith argues that in the narrator's transition from tenderfoot to veteran in *Roughing It*, the Western travel narrative "has for the first time acquired a moral significance. . . . The standard by which good is distinguished from bad and wisdom from foolishness, is no longer to be found in the settled society which the traveler is on the point of leaving behind but resides in that as-yet-unknown Far West toward which his journey is taking him." The hero is "the vernacular character, outside the official culture and with no apparent stake in it," though even Professor Smith admits that the "exact content of the vernacular values is not made clear." Persuasive as this reading is, and useful as it is in interpreting aspects of Mark Twain's writings, it overlooks, I believe, the variety of

Mark Twain's attitudes toward the West in *Roughing It*, his complex identification with both vernacular values and those of the official culture, his ability to stand aside—in a third position, as it were—and contrast those values for humor, and his tendency to push the conventional to an extreme where it becomes an easy target for satire and humor.

Mark Twain and the Myth of the Daring Jest (Brodwin)

1. In *My Mark Twain: Reminiscences and Criticism*, ed. and with an introduction by Marilyn Austin Baldwin (Baton Rouge: Louisiana State University Press, 1967), p. 87.

2. See V. L. Parrington, "The Back-Wash of the Frontier—Mark Twain," in *The Beginnings of Critical Realism in America* (New York: Harcourt, Brace, 1930), pp. 86–101. Of course, much of the Brooks–DeVoto controversy centered on this issue, and though Parrington reflects DeVoto's position that the frontier shaped and fulfilled Twain's art, modern criticism has tended to synthesize both sides. Still the best summary is Lewis Leary's introduction to his *Mark Twain's Wound: A Casebook*, ed. Lewis Leary (New York: Crowell, 1962).

3. See the review reprinted in *Pudd'nhead Wilson and Those Extraordinary Twins: Authoritative Texts; Textual Notes; Criticism*, ed. Sidney E. Berger (New York: W. W. Norton, 1980), pp. 216–17.

4. *The Writings of Mark Twain*, ed. A. B. Paine, 37 vols. (New York: Harper & Brothers, 1923), vol. 13. All references will be to this Stormfield edition, unless otherwise noted.

5. See David E. E. Sloane's study, *Mark Twain as a Literary Comedian* (Baton Rouge: Louisiana State University Press, 1979), which analyzes how Twain surpassed his fellow humorists in style and vision. As early as 1866, Bret Harte, with whom Twain "competed," recognized that Twain's "certain hearty abhorrence of shams will make his faculty serviceable to mankind. His talent is so well based that he can write seriously and well when he chooses, which is perhaps the best test of true humor." Quoted in Margaret Duckett, *Mark Twain and Bret Harte* (Norman: University of Oklahoma Press, 1964), p. 28.

6. *Prejudices, Second Series* (New York: Knopf, 1920), pp. 52–53.

7. See *Mark Twain's Quarrel with God*, ed. Ray B. Browne (New Haven, Conn., College & University Press, 1970), p. 30. According to Browne, the story was written in Germany during the winter of 1891–92. References to the story will be to this edition.

8. The standard treatment of the subject is Allison Ensor, *Mark Twain & the Bible* (Lexington: University of Kentucky Press, 1969). See also

Stanley Brodwin, "The Humor of the Absurd: Mark Twain's Adamic Diaries," *Criticism*, 15 (Winter 1972), 49–64, and "The Theology of Mark Twain: Banished Adam and the Bible," *Mississippi Quarterly*, 29 (Spring 1976), 167–89. Twain's biblical "complex" dynamically informed his comic modes and ideas, even as he desperately tried to emancipate himself from its influence on him.

9. Quoted in Jeffrey R. Holland, "Soul-Butter and Hogwash: Mark Twain and Frontier Religion," in *Soul-Butter and Hog Wash and Other Essays on the American West*, ed. Thomas G. Alexander (Provo, Utah: Brigham Young University Press, 1978), p. 14. Other helpful studies on Twain's "religion" are John Q. Hays, "Mark Twain's Rebellion against God: Origins," *Southwestern American Literature*, 3 (1973), 27–38; Lloyd A. Hunter, "Mark Twain and the Southern Evangelical Mind," *Bulletin of the Missouri Historical Society*, 33 (July 1977), 246–64; and John T. Frederick, *The Darkened Sky: Nineteenth Century American Novelists & Religion* (Notre Dame, Ind.: University of Notre Dame Press, 1969), chap. 4. Frederick correctly points out that of all our major novelists, Mark Twain "was the most outspoken in his reactions to the religious tensions of his time" (p. 123).

10. See Letter XI, 2 March 1867, in *Mark Twain's Travels with Mr. Brown*, ed. Franklin Walker and G. Ezra Dane (1940 rpt.; New York: Russell & Russell, 1971), pp. 114–15.

11. In the "... Remains of George Holland by the Rev. Mr. Sabine" (1871), in *What Is Man? and Other Philosophical Writings*, ed. with an introduction by Paul Baender (Berkeley: University of California Press, 1973), p. 53. Baender's introduction gives an expert description of Twain's religious "values" and prints the many short, angry pieces Twain wrote on religious hypocrisy. Twain recognized that the "blamed wildcat religions" (p. 40) of his time only made the problem more difficult for an honest preacher or writer to overcome.

12. But see the many pieces on the "Myth of Providence" in *Mark Twain's Fables of Man*, ed. with an introduction by John S. Tuckey (Berkeley: University of California Press, 1972). Also consult Robert Lee Cody's helpful (unpublished) Ph.D. dissertation, "Providence in the Novels of Mark Twain" (University of Florida, 1978).

13. See Joe Lee Davis, "Mystical versus Enthusiastic Sensibility," *Journal of the History of Ideas*, 43 (June 1943), 301–20, which shows how the idea of Providence became particularly vital as a weapon against the growing antireligious thought of the seventeenth century.

14. C. Merton Babcock, in his "Mark Twain and the Freedom to Tell a Lie," *Texas Quarterly*, 5 (August 1962), 155–60, quotes many examples from every phase of Twain's work and offers an interesting analysis of how

the "need" to lie was turned to his psychological and artistic advantage. See also Eric Solomon's "*Huckleberry Finn* Once More," *College English*, 18 (December 1960), 172–78, an insightful look at the ways Huck's lies define his search for identity.

15. *My Mark Twain*, p. 77.

16. In "The Turning Point of My Life" (1910), 27:139–40.

17. In "The Character of Man" (1885), p. 61, in *What Is Man? and Other Philosophical Writings*. This piece appeared first in Twain's *Autobiography* (ed. A. B. Paine), 2:7–13. It contains a "satanic" description of the pervasiveness of lies in every aspect of man's existence, leaving him to do "his little dirt," die, and "send no messages back—selfish even in death" (p. 64).

18. See Edgar M. Branch, "The Two Providences: Thematic Form in *Huckleberry Finn*," *College English*, 11 (1950), 188–95.

19. Twain used this phrase in describing himself in a letter to Howells after Susy's death. See *Mark Twain–Howells Letters*, ed. Henry Nash Smith and William M. Gibson (Cambridge, Mass.: Harvard University Press, 1960), 2:664–65. I analyze the implications of this image in my article, "Mark Twain's Masks of Satan: The Final Phase," *American Literature*, 45 (May 1973), 217ff. All references to the Mysterious Stranger stories will be to *Mark Twain's Mysterious Stranger Manuscripts*, ed. and with an introduction by William Gibson (Berkeley: University of California Press, 1969). Recent studies of these stories are in Sholom Kahn, *Mark Twain's Mysterious Stranger* (Columbia: University of Missouri Press, 1978), and William Macnaughton, *Mark Twain's Last Years as a Writer* (Columbia: University of Missouri Press, 1979).

20. For an excellent study of Joan in Twain's work, see William Searle, *The Saint & the Skeptics: Joan of Arc in the Works of Mark Twain, Anatole France, and Bernard Shaw* (Detroit: Wayne State University Press, 1976). Also see James D. Wilson, "In Quest of Redemptive Vision: Mark Twain's *Joan of Arc*," *Texas Studies in Literature and Language*, 20 (Summer 1978), 181–98.

21. Quoted in Marie Collins Swabey, *Comic Laughter: A Philosophical Essay* (New Haven: Yale University Press, 1961), p. 96. My discussion here is indebted to this brilliant study.

22. Quoted in Swabey, *Comic Laughter*, from Kierkegaard's *Concluding Unscientific Postscript*, p. 96.

23. For an analysis of these modes of irony, see Gregor Malantschuk, *Kierkegaard's Thought*, trans. Howard and Edna Hong (Princeton: Princeton University Press, 1971), pp. 201ff. And in his *Journals*, Kierkegaard wrote: "This world is a world of untruth, of lies, and to live Christianity in it means to suffer." In *Soren Kierkegaard's Journals and Papers*, ed. How-

ard V. Hong and Edna H. Hong (Bloomington: Indiana University Press, 1967), 1A-E:63. No doubt Mark Twain would have fully endorsed this statement, as well as Kierkegaard's indictment of Christianity's loss of genuine faith.

24. Quoted in Gibson in his introduction to *Mark Twain's Mysterious Stranger Manuscripts*, p. 26.

25. "The Chronicle of Young Satan," in ibid., pp. 165–66.

26. See Dewey Ganzel, *Mark Twain Abroad: The Cruise of the Quaker City* (Chicago: University of Chicago Press, 1968). It is true, as Ganzel points out, that many "sardonic" portraits of some of the passengers remained in the final text, but Twain had nevertheless made the voyage seem like "fun" (p. 299). In the end, the critical uproar was about the book's "irreverent" attitude toward the hallowed past, a reflex cultural reaction that ignored the work's "serious" intentions in content and style. See Philip D. Beidler, "Realistic Style and the Problem of Context in *Innocents Abroad* and *Roughing It*," *American Quarterly*, 52 (March 1980), 33–49, for an excellent study of those intentions.

27. I develop this interpretation in my article, "The Useful & the Useless River: *Life on the Mississippi* Revisited," *Studies in American Humor*, 2 (January 1976), 196–208.

28. In "On the Essence of Laughter" in *The Painter of Modern Life and Other Essays*, trans. and ed. by Jonathan Mayne (London: Phaidon Press, 1964), p. 148. I have already touched upon the relationship of Twain's theological view of humor to Baudelaire's in my "The Humor of the Absurd: Mark Twain's Adamic Diaries" (see note 8 above). Laughter only exists in a "fallen" state, where contradictions abound. The comic artist laughs with fear and trembling at the horror of that condition.

29. Everett Carter's "The Meaning of *A Connecticut Yankee*," *American Literature*, 50 (November 1978), 418–40, summarizes the "soft" and "hard" attitudes taken by critics toward the book. Carter argues persuasively that Hank's "longing is not for a pretechnological Eden, but for an England that the Yankee, like Robinson Crusoe, has made bearable by the exercise of his ingenuity" (p. 439).

30. In *Mark Twain's Which Was the Dream? and Other Symbolical Writings of the Later Years*, ed. with an introduction by John S. Tuckey (Berkeley: University of California Press, 1967), p. 515. This kind of "humor" pervades the work, even to reducing Twain's comic and literary heritage to various microbes flowing in his "ancestral" blood. Thus Lemuel Gulliver is *"Head of the Pus-Breeders,"* Colonel Sellers gives *"Lockjaw,"* and Don Quixote causes *"Recurrent Fever"* (pp. 471–72).

31. The idea of God's responsibility appears in many of Twain's works, e.g., the Adamic Diaries; *Letters from the Earth*, ed. Bernard DeVoto

(New York: Harper & Row, 1962); and in "Reflections on Religion," ed. Charles Neider, *Hudson Review*, 16 (Autumn 1963), 329–52.

32. Salvador de Madariaga in *Don Quixote: An Introductory Essay in Psychology* (London: Oxford University Press, 1935) shows clearly how Quixote and Sancho gradually adopt each other's attitudes.

33. Two important works that deal with the idea of "innocence" in Twain's thought are Albert E. Stone, *The Innocent Eye: Childhood in the Imagination of Mark Twain* (New Haven: Yale University Press, 1961), and William C. Spengemann, *Mark Twain and the Backwoods Angel* (Kent, Ohio: Kent State University Press, 1966). Strictly speaking, of course, there is no *true* innocence in Twain's fallen world (except in the Adamic diaries, which dramatize the Fall). There is only a constructed Adamic stance which generates a mediating humor between its possibilities of freedom or "salvation" and the gradual awareness of their loss.

Contributors

PHILIP D. BEIDLER, Associate Professor of English at The University of Alabama, was co-director of the 1981 Twain Symposium and is the author of *American Literature and the Experience of Vietnam*. He is working on a companion study concerning the youth literature of the 1960s and 1970s.

STANLEY BRODWIN is Professor of English at Hofstra University. His many published articles on Twain's Adamic Diaries and the Satanic mode in his work have culminated in a book he is preparing on theological themes in Twain's writings.

LOUIS J. BUDD, Professor of English at Duke University, has written *Mark Twain: Social Philosopher*; *Robert Herrick*; and *A Listing of and Selection from Newspaper and Magazine Interviews with Samuel L. Clemens, 1874–1910*. With Edwin H. Cady and Carl Anderson he edited *Toward a New American Literary History: Essays in Honor of Arlin Turner*. In addition to editing two volumes on Twain, *Critical Essays on Mark Twain, 1867–1910* and *Critical Essays on Mark Twain, 1910–1980*, he has also recently published *Our Mark Twain: The Making of His Public Personality*.

JAMES M. COX, Professor of English at Dartmouth College, is the author of *Twentieth Century Views: Robert Frost* and *Mark Twain: The Fate of Humor*.

178

SARA DESAUSSURE DAVIS, Associate Professor of English at The University of Alabama, was co-director of the Twain Symposium of 1981, and is the author of articles on Henry James and Kate Chopin. She is working now on Kate Chopin's unpublished collection, "A Vocation and A Voice."

ALLISON R. ENSOR, Professor of English at the University of Tennessee, Knoxville, is the author of *Mark Twain and the Bible* and editor of the Norton Critical Edition of *A Connecticut Yankee in King Arthur's Court*. An essay on the illustrating of *Huckleberry Finn* is forthcoming in *Adventures of Huckleberry Finn: Centenary Essays*.

JOHN C. GERBER, Professor of English at State University of New York at Albany, is the co-editor of a variety of text books, including *The College Teaching of English, Better Reading, Factual Prose, Literature, Writers Resource Book, Speakers Resource Book, Toward Better Writing*, and *Repertory*. He has also compiled and edited two collections of criticism, *Twentieth Century Interpretations of The Scarlet Letter* and *Studies in Huckleberry Finn*. In addition to chairing the Editorial Board of the Iowa-California Edition of the Works of Mark Twain, he has co-edited *The Adventures of Tom Sawyer; Tom Sawyer Abroad; Tom Sawyer, Detective*. He is completing a volume on Mark Twain in the Twayne series.

ALAN GRIBBEN is Associate Professor of English at the University of Texas, Austin. His ten-year study of Twain's library and reading has resulted in a two-volume work, *Mark Twain's Library: A Reconstruction*. He has recently edited a burlesque poem, *Mark Twain's Rubáiyát* and is completing a supplement to *Mark Twain's Library* as well as finishing a book-length study of prevalent patterns in Twain's writings.

HAROLD H. KOLB is Professor of English at the Unversity of Virginia. His books include *The Illusion of Life: American Realism as a Literary Form; A Field Guide to the Study of American Literature;* and *A Writer's Guide: The Essential Points*. He is currently working on a book titled "Mark Twain as Humorist."

HENRY NASH SMITH, Professor Emeritus since 1974 of the University of California, Berkeley, has written *Virgin Land: The American West as Symbol and Myth*; *Mark Twain: The Development of a Writer*; *Mark Twain's Fable of Progress*; and *Democracy and the Novel: Popular Resistance to Classic American Writers*. He has edited *Mark Twain of the "Enterprise," Mark Twain-Howells Letters* (with William M. Gibson), and *Popular Culture and Industrialism, 1865–90*.

Index